DIGITAL MARKETING

FOR HOME SERVICE BUSINESSES

Lead Generation Tactics for
Appliance Repair, HVAC, Electrical,
and Plumbing

Micheal A. Carson

Digital Marketing for Home Service Businesses

Disclaimer

The information provided in this book is for general informational purposes only. While the author has endeavored to provide accurate and up-to-date information, no representation or warranty is made as to the accuracy or completeness of the contents of this book. The author and publisher disclaim any liability in connection with the use of this information.

ISBN: 9798332612619

Independently published by Michael A. Carson on Kindle Direct Publishing

First Edition, 2025

CONTENTS

Acknowledgements 1

Introduction 5

Chapter 1: Setting the Digital Marketing Foundation.......17

Chapter 2: Building a Robust Online Presence 25

Chapter 3: SEO for Home Service Companies..................57

Chapter 4: Content Marketing 69

Chapter 5: Social Media Marketing 81

Chapter 6: Google Business Profile Optimization..............99

Chapter 7: Cracking the Google Ads Code...................117

Chapter 8: Email Marketing 135

Chapter 9: A Pep Talk from Your Coach 151

Chapter 10: Analytics and Monitoring.............................153

Chapter 11: Automation and AI in Marketing.................167

Chapter 12: Scaling Your Marketing Efforts 183

Chapter 13: Advanced SEO Techniques.........................195

Chapter 14: A Case Study Of Success............................247

Chapter 15: Next Steps 255

Chapter 16: Appendices 259

ACKNOWLEDGEMENTS

I wanted to take a moment right up front to thank a few people that helped make this book possible. Without these people, this book would have never come to fruition.

First and foremost, I want to give praise to God for His sovereign love, guidance, and grace. As a Christian, my faith is the foundation of my life, and without it, I would not be the man I am today. I am eternally grateful for the strength, wisdom, and purpose that my relationship with God provides.

I want to express my deepest gratitude to my loving wife, Cathy, and our 3 incredible children. Your unwavering support, encouragement, patience, and understanding during the long hours and late nights of work, continuous learning, and personal growth over the past two decades were invaluable. I love you all more than words can say.

To my partners at Service Alliance Group, TK, Zack, and EJ. I thank you for bringing me on board this amazing journey, and allowing me to be a part of something much bigger than myself. Thank you for fostering an environment that encourages creativity, innovation, and the pursuit of knowledge. I absolutely love what we've been able to build together that helps so many home service business owners organize, manage, and scale their businesses - providing a pathway to stability and freedom.

And to the broader Service Alliance Community, your collective wisdom and shared experiences have enriched my perspective and greatly contributed to the ideas and concepts expressed in this book.

I am also deeply indebted to my closest personal friends, Joe, Rob/Dawn, and Matt/LeAnn, whose belief in me and my work has been a constant source of inspiration and encouragement. Your willingness to listen, offer feedback, and celebrate milestones (both big and small) has made this journey all the more rewarding. I enjoy doing life with you and thank God every day for bringing us together.

To my extraordinary team at Appliance Marketing Pros, your talent, dedication, and collaborative spirit are the driving force behind everything we achieve. I am continually inspired by your creativity, your technical expertise, and your unwavering commitment to delivering exceptional results for our clients. Thank you for your tireless efforts, your willingness to embrace new challenges, and your unwavering belief in the power of digital marketing to transform businesses. I am honored to work alongside each and every one of you.

To our valued clients, past and present, thank you for partnering with us on your digital journeys. Your trust in our expertise and your willingness to embrace new strategies have been instrumental in our own growth and development. We are inspired by your unique brands, your ambitious goals, and your unwavering commitment to connecting with your audiences in meaningful ways. Your challenges have pushed us to innovate, and your successes have fueled our passion for this ever-evolving field. We are truly grateful for the opportunity to collaborate with you, and we look forward to continuing to achieve remarkable results together in the digital landscape.

INTRODUCTION

Thank you for picking up your copy of "**Digital Marketing for Home Service Businesses.**"

You have chosen to elevate your business in the competitive home service industry by reading this book. You can dominate your local market with a tailored approach to help you dominate your industry, whether you're in appliance repair, HVAC, electrical, plumbing or any other home service industry.

There are a lot of strategies out there for digital marketing, including search engine optimization, pay-per-click advertising, social media marketing, and more. In this book, you'll learn how to boost your online presence, generate more leads, and ultimately grow your revenue by breaking down these complex concepts into actionable steps that you can implement right away.

What You'll Discover Inside:

- **A Comprehensive Marketing Blueprint:** We start with the fundamentals and gradually progress to advanced tactics, ensuring you understand digital marketing principles.

- **Optimizing Conversions:** Use effective conversion strategies to transform your website visitors into loyal customers.

- **SEO Techniques:** Learn the art of search engine optimization. Enhance your visibility and attract more traffic with keyword research and link building.

- **Local SEO Mastery:** Essential strategies to boost your presence in local search results and enhance your credibility through Google Business Profile and reviews.

- **Engaging Content Creation:** Produce informative blog posts and captivating videos that resonate with your audience.

- **Social Media Savvy:** Harness the power of social platforms to engage potential customers, build your brand, and drive traffic.

- **Effective Paid Advertising:** Learn the nuances of pay-per-click advertising, Google Ads, and social media campaigns to ensure your marketing dollars work harder for you.

- **Email Marketing Excellence:** Craft targeted email campaigns and automate follow-ups to convert leads and retain customers.

- **Online Reputation Management:** Ways of building and maintaining your online reputation through positive reviews and addressing feedback effectively.

- **Analytics and Data-Driven Decisions:** Make informed decisions based on analytics tools to track performance.

- **Embracing Automation and AI:** Learn how to enhance customer interactions and streamline your marketing efforts.

The goal of this book is not just to offer a guide, but also to provide a roadmap for home service businesses to succeed in the digital age. By following the strategies outlined here, you'll be well-equipped to navigate the complexities of digital marketing, outperform your competitors, and achieve sustainable growth for your company.

Let's transform your business into a digital powerhouse. Let's make your success story a reality.

About The Author

Before we dive in, let me introduce myself and explain why my advice in this book is worth your time. My name is Mike Carson, and I've been immersed in the world of digital marketing for over 20 years.

I started my digital marketing career in September 2004 with a simple objective: to help small business owners grow their businesses and achieve their goals through effective digital strategies. As the lead Marketing Strategist and SEO Specialist, I've had the privilege of working with a diverse range of clients— from small businesses worldwide to Fortune 500 companies and even celebrity clientele. My passion for this field has also led me to become a frequent speaker and trainer at digital marketing, SEO, and home services conferences. Along the way, I've won several web design and SEO awards, showcasing the effectiveness of my research and SEO testing methods.

My true passion lies in helping home service businesses, like yours, achieve their digital marketing goals. At my agency, **ApplianceMarketingPros.com**, my team and I specialize in highly optimized web design, search engine optimization, and comprehensive digital marketing strategies. We're a dedicated group of web designers, SEO specialists, content writers, and Google Ads experts, all committed to driving your success.

I'm also one of the co-founders of **Service Alliance Group**, an association that supports home service companies. We help business owners in the appliance repair, HVAC, electrical, and plumbing fields, offering them community, coaching, and resources to help organize, manage, and scale their businesses, providing a pathway to stability and freedom. You can find out more about Service Alliance Group by going to https://servicealliancegroup.com.

Additionally, I co-host the **Service Alliance Group Podcast**, and host my own **Local Marketing Lounge Podcast** on YouTube, where I share insights and strategies to help you navigate the digital marketing landscape. So, trust me when I say, the advice in this book comes from years of hands-on experience and a genuine commitment to seeing your home service business thrive. You'll find the links to these podcasts in the appendix at the end of this book.

The Importance of Digital Marketing for Home Service Companies

Digital marketing has become an essential part of the survival and success of home service companies in today's fast-paced, technologically advanced world. Traditional marketing methods are still relevant, but more is needed when reaching a tech-savvy audience seeking answers online. Homeowners can find information about your appliance repair, HVAC, electrical, or plumbing services with one click. By embracing digital marketing, businesses can increase their visibility, build credibility, and engage with a wider audience. By establishing a strong online presence, businesses can reach potential customers where they spend most of their time: online.

Digital marketing allows home service companies to attract and convert leads. Effective SEO practices help businesses appear at the top of search results when customers seek local services. Building trust and showcasing expertise through engaging content, whether posted on blogs, social media platforms, or via video, is imperative. A strong Google Business Profile and online reviews further enhance a company's reputation, ensuring that potential clients will feel comfortable choosing their services. A home service company can build long-term relationships with its customers and generate steady leads through these digital channels.

Digital marketing also provides businesses valuable insight and data that help them continually refine their marketing strategies. Analytics tools monitor key performance metrics, helping them know what works and doesn't. Through this data-driven approach, home service providers can optimize their marketing efforts for maximum ROI, ensuring that each dollar they spend contributes to their growth and success. Staying ahead in a competitive market means embracing these advanced marketing techniques to survive, outshine your competitors, and establish a prosperous future.

Overview of Appliance Repair, HVAC, Plumbing, and Electrical Industries

Even in economic uncertainty, the home service industry, including appliance repair, HVAC, plumbing, and electrical services, is growing and thriving. A Harris Williams Home Services Study found that nearly half of consumers (49%) spend more on home services than they did two to three years ago. There are several factors contributing to this trend, including a growing desire for do-it-for-me services, the aging population requiring more professional assistance, and millennials buying homes who prefer to have home-related tasks outsourced. Taking advantage of these dynamics presents an enormous opportunity for home service companies to expand their market reach and differentiate themselves through professionalization and sophisticated marketing. This growing demand can only be captured through digital marketing.

According to the study, consumers are more likely to find and evaluate home service providers through digital channels. Word-of-mouth plays a significant role, with reputation, quality, and price still top priorities. There has, however, been an increase in the importance of online presence, as internet searches, online reviews, and social media have become critical discovery and validation resources for homeowners. The number of consumers who expect service providers to use technology for billing, booking, and communication management has increased to nearly two-thirds. The urgency of investing in digital marketing for home service businesses to remain competitive and meet evolving customer expectations cannot be overstated. Modern consumers expect companies to offer convenience and transparency, so those that fully leverage digital marketing effectively benefit from building strong local reputations, engaging with today's tech-savvy customers, and building strong local reputations.

Interesting Stats You Should Know

When consumers look for home service repair providers or service contractors, they often turn to their phones to make inquiries and requests. Despite the common practice of seeking multiple estimates, nearly half of consumers only consider one local contractor before making a decision. This underscores the importance of making a strong first impression and converting phone leads promptly.

Unfortunately, about a third of home service and contractor business calls go unanswered, leading to significant lost business opportunities. Here are some eye-opening statistics that highlight the critical role of phone calls in the home services and construction industries:

Home Services & Contractor Businesses Depend on Calls to Grow Revenue

- **70%** of appointments for appliance repair are initiated through inbound calls (Invoca).

- **76%** of pest control shoppers make a call after searching online (Local Search Association - LSA).

- **80%** of plumbing appointments come from inbound calls (Invoca).

- **84%** of homeowners looking for roofing services call after an online search (LSA).

- **40%** of people only consider one local contractor before making a decision (Google).

- **60%** of consumers prefer to call a home services business before purchasing (Invoca).

- **40%** of consumers avoid calling home services businesses due to long hold times (Invoca).

- **47%** of home service business calls are potential leads (Invoca).

- **30%** of home services phone leads result in conversions (Invoca).

- **27%** of calls to home services businesses go unanswered (Invoca).

Expanding on These Findings

The Importance of Answering Calls

A significant portion of business in the home services sector is driven by phone calls. For example, **70%** of appointments for appliance repair and **80%** of plumbing appointments come from inbound calls. This indicates that consumers heavily rely on phone communications to engage with service providers. Moreover, **60%** of consumers say they will call a home services business before making a purchase, emphasizing the need for businesses to be readily available over the phone.

Lost Opportunities Due to Unanswered Calls

The report reveals that **27%** of calls to home services businesses are unanswered, which translates to many missed business opportunities. With **30%** of home services phone leads converting, businesses potentially lose significant revenue by not answering calls.

Consumer Behavior and Preferences

The statistic that **40%** of people only consider one local contractor before making a decision highlights the importance of being the first to respond to a consumer's inquiry. Additionally, **40%** of consumers avoid calling home services businesses due to long hold times, indicating that improving call-handling processes could increase customer engagement and conversions.

A Blunt Reminder Before Getting Too Deep

I have to be very blunt about something before you get any deeper into this book. Some of you out there need to hear this **loud and clear**! If you're not going to answer your phone, there's no need to worry about any marketing strategies at this time. You can put down this book, set it on a shelf right now, and **fuggetaboutit**. The strategies in this book are designed to bring you more leads and phone calls. If you can't handle the call volume you currently have, what makes you think you can handle even more?

Simply put, you can significantly increase your revenue by answering 100% of your phone calls. So, pick up that phone and start converting those leads! If you're already set with a dedicated CSR or outsourcing your call management, then kudos to you, read on and lets get this digital marketing party started.

CHAPTER

1

SETTING THE DIGITAL MARKETING FOUNDATION

The first step towards long-term success is to lay down the essential foundations of digital marketing. Basically, you need to build a solid foundation for a house. If you do not, anything built on top will be unstable. The fundamental elements of effective digital marketing also align with this concept. All of this will make sense and be clear to you by the end of this chapter.

First, in order to chart a clear path to achieving your goals and objectives, I'll help you define them. Setting precise objectives will keep you focused and guide your marketing efforts, whether you're aiming to increase traffic to your website, generate more leads, or improve your brand's online reputation.

Next, we'll move on to identifying your target audience. Understanding who your ideal customers are is key to creating marketing strategies that resonate with them. Your audience plays a crucial role in this process, and we'll explore how to gather insights about them, segment them effectively, and tailor your messaging to meet their needs and preferences.

Last but not least, we will discuss how to establish measurable KPIs (Key Performance Indicators). This is not just a set of numbers but your guiding light. It will help you determine your marketing campaign's success and track your progress. You can optimize your strategies and ensure that every marketing dollar contributes to your overall goals by setting clear KPIs, which allow you to make data-driven decisions.

By the end of this chapter, you'll have a comprehensive blueprint for your digital marketing strategy. Let's start laying a solid foundation for your digital marketing efforts by determining what you want to achieve, who you need to reach, and how you can measure your results.

Defining Your Goals and Objectives

Home service companies must set clear goals and objectives to succeed with digital marketing. If you set clear goals, your marketing efforts can become smooth and focused and save time and effort. Your goals guide your strategies and ensure that your actions align with your business goals. As a home service company, you can increase brand awareness in your local area, drive more leads to your website, or improve customer satisfaction. You need clear goals to stay on track and measure your progress to adjust your strategies effectively.

Here are actionable steps to help you establish clear and attainable goals for your home service company:

1. **Identify Your Business Goals:** Start by listing the overarching goals of your business. These could include increasing brand awareness, boosting sales, growing your customer base, or entering new markets.

2. **Align Marketing Goals with Business Goals:** Ensure that your digital marketing objectives align with your broader business goals. For instance, if your business goal is to increase sales, your marketing goal might be to generate more qualified leads.

3. **Make Your Goals SMART:** SMART goals are Specific, Measurable, Achievable, Relevant, and Time-bound. For example, instead of saying "increase website traffic," a SMART goal would be "increase website traffic by 25% over the next six months."

4. **Prioritize Your Goals:** Not all goals are equal in importance. Prioritize them based on their potential impact on your business.

5. **Document and Communicate Your Goals:** Write down your goals and share them with your team. This ensures everyone is on the same page and working towards the same objectives.

Identifying Your Target Audience

Your marketing efforts can be tailored to meet your ideal customers' specific needs and preferences for home service companies if you know who your ideal customers are. You will be able to reach the right people with the right message, improving the effectiveness of your campaigns. You can increase the likelihood of leads becoming loyal customers by focusing your resources on the most promising prospects and identifying your target audience.

How to Identify Your Target Audience

Examine your current customers to identify common characteristics, such as demographics, location, and service preferences. This can provide valuable insights into who is already using your services.

1. **Establish Buyer Personas:** Develop detailed profiles of your ideal customers, incorporating age, gender, income level, job title, interests, and pain points. You will be able to better understand their needs through this process.

2. **Market Research:** Use surveys, interviews, and online research to learn more about your potential customers. Google Analytics and social media insights can also provide valuable demographic information.

3. **Segment Your Audience:** Divide your audience into smaller groups based on specific criteria such as location, behavior, or service needs. By doing so, marketing campaigns can be more targeted and personalized.

4. **Monitor Competitor Activity:** Analyze who your competitors are targeting and how. You can use this to identify potential market gaps and refine your audience targeting.

5. **Test and Refine:** Continuously test different marketing messages and strategies with different audience segments. Make improvements to your approach based on the results of your research.

Setting Measurable KPIs

Your digital marketing efforts can be tracked using KPIs (Key Performance Indicators). KPIs provide quantifiable measurements of how well your marketing strategies perform against your goals. This data-driven approach ensures you make informed decisions that drive growth and efficiency by understanding what's working, what's not, and where to improve for home service companies.

How to Set Up Measurable KPIs

1. **Align KPIs with Your Goals:** Ensure each KPI is directly tied to your specific digital marketing goals. For instance, if your aim is to boost website traffic, a relevant KPI could be the number of new visitors to your site.

2. **Choose Relevant KPIs:** Select meaningful key performance indicators (KPIs) and gain insight into

your marketing performance. Avoid using superficial metrics that do not directly contribute to your business objectives.

3. **Make KPIs Specific and Measurable:** Your KPIs should be clear and quantifiable. Instead of a general metric like "increase engagement," specify "increase social media engagement rate by 15%."

4. **Use a Mix of KPIs:** Keep an eye on various KPIs to get a full picture of your performance. Track metrics for reach, engagement, conversion, and customer satisfaction.

5. **Set Benchmarks:** Establish baseline metrics to compare your KPIs against. This will help you understand your starting point and measure progress over time.

6. **Regularly Review and Adjust:** Monitor your key performance indicators (KPIs) and adjust your strategies based on the insights gained to ensure continuous improvement and optimization of your marketing efforts.

Key KPIs to Track

- **Website Traffic:** Number of visitors, unique visitors, and page views.

- **Conversion Rate:** Percentage of visitors who complete a desired action (e.g., filling out a form, booking a service).

- **Bounce Rate:** Percentage of visitors who leave your site after viewing only one page.

- **Social Media Engagement:** Likes, comments, shares, and follower growth on social media platforms.

- **Lead Generation:** Number of new leads acquired through your digital marketing efforts.

- **Customer Acquisition Cost (CAC):** Total cost of acquiring a new customer.

- **Return on Investment (ROI):** Revenue generated from your marketing activities compared to the costs incurred.

- **Online Reviews and Ratings:** Number and quality of online reviews and ratings.

- **Email Open and Click-Through Rates:** Engagement metrics for your email marketing campaigns.

- **Customer Retention Rate:** Percentage of customers who return for repeat services.

2

BUILDING A ROBUST ONLINE PRESENCE

Our focus in this chapter is on building an online presence that will be the foundation of your entire digital marketing strategy. In today's world, your online presence is your biggest asset. Unfortunately, many home service companies fall short in this area and often choose to "go cheap," which can significantly undermine their success more than they realize. An effective online presence is more than just a website; it's about creating a user-friendly, professional, and optimized digital business asset that drives traffic and converts leads.

Did you realize that a poorly developed website can negatively affect all of these things?

- Your Google Business Profile Rankings

- Your Google Ads quality scores and the amount you spend on ads

- Your organic search engine rankings

- Your user engagement and retention

- Your conversion rates and lead generation

- Your online reputation and customer trust

- Your site's loading speed and overall performance

- Your mobile responsiveness and accessibility

- Your social media sharing and visibility

- Your ability to track and analyze user behavior with analytics tools

- **Your INCOME!**

Not to mention your competition is probably laughing at you while they cash in on all those extra leads they got because your website just plain sucks, and theirs doesn't.

Designing a professional website is the first step in building a digital presence for your business and the first impression potential customers will have of your services. A well-designed website attracts visitors and instills trust and credibility, making them more likely to choose you over your competitors. I'll walk you through the essential elements that make a website good and exceptional so your visitors will choose your business over your competitors.

With most homeowners using smartphones and tablets to access websites, ensuring your site looks great on all devices is crucial. A mobile-responsive website not only caters to the needs of your audience but also boosts your search engine rankings, reduces bounce rates, and enhances user experience. This adaptability is key to staying competitive in the digital landscape.

We'll then discuss User Experience and Conversion Optimization. You need more than visitors to your website; you need them to become customers and leads. Whether you want them to fill out a contact form, schedule a service, or make a phone call, I'll teach you how to create a seamless user experience that guides visitors to take the desired actions.

Our final topic will be Mastering Website Optimization for Search Engines. Your online presence depends on search engine optimization (SEO), which means your website will appear high in search results when potential customers look for your services. Using keyword research and technical SEO, we'll guide you through optimizing your website to increase organic traffic to your site.

By the end of this chapter, you'll have a comprehensive understanding of what it takes to build and maintain a strong online presence. This chapter will show you why investing in these aspects is beneficial and essential to the growth and sustainability of your home service business in the long term. Let's create a unique online presence that will drive your business forward.

Designing a Professional Website

Choosing the Right Platform

If you plan to build a professional website for your home service company, choose the right platform. WordPress is flexible and scalable and has many plugins and themes to meet your needs. Unlike DIY website builders, WordPress allows you to build a robust online presence more easily because you have more control over its design and functionality.

Why DIY Website Builders Are Not the Best Choice

Due to their ease of use and low cost, DIY website builders such as Wix, Squarespace, and GoDaddy Website Builder may seem appealing, but they often have significant limitations. You may not have the ability to fully customize your website, integrate advanced features, and fully optimize it for SEO. As a result, your website may not stand out in a competitive market because it lacks professionalism and functionality. If you invest in a custom WordPress site, you have a unique, fully functional website that can grow as your business does.

PRO TIP: Avoid using DIY website builders at all costs.

There is proven SEO research available that shows DIY website platforms perform poorly compared to self hosted CMS platforms such as WordPress.

Essential Elements for a Professional Home Service Company Website

1. **High-Quality Images**

   - **Why It Matters:** High-quality images create a strong first impression and convey professionalism. Photos of your team, equipment, and completed projects help build trust and showcase the quality of your work.

2. **Clear and Easy-to-Read Logo**

   - **Why It Matters:** Your brand identity starts with your logo. You should display your brand logo prominently and make it easily identifiable so your customers can remember it.

3. **Use of Brand Colors**

   - **Why It Matters:** Visually appealing websites use consistent brand colors to reinforce their identity. It helps create a cohesive look and feel that customers associate with your business.

4. **Click-to-Call Phone Numbers**

   - **Why It Matters:** Many customers will visit your site on mobile devices. Click-to-call phone numbers make it easy for them to contact you directly, improving the chances of converting visitors into leads.

5. **Call-to-Action Buttons**

   - **Why It Matters:** For visitors to take specific actions, call-to-action buttons are needed. For instance, a quote request button directs visitors toward scheduling a service call. CTAs must be clear, compelling, and easy to understand to increase conversion rates.

6. **Easy Scheduling for Customers**

   - **Why It Matters:** An intuitive scheduling system allows customers to book services conveniently, reducing friction and increasing the likelihood of securing their business.

7. Customer Reviews

- **Why It Matters:** Displaying customer reviews builds credibility and trust. Positive reviews from other customers will encourage potential clients to choose your services.

8. Service Pages for Each Service

- **Why It Matters:** Dedicated pages for each service you offer provide detailed information and improve SEO. It helps customers find exactly what they're looking for and understand the range of services you provide.

9. City Pages for Major Service Areas

- **Why It Matters:** Creating pages for each city or town you service helps you rank higher in local search results. It also shows customers that you are a local expert who understands their needs.

10. About Us Page

- **Why It Matters:** An engaging About Us page humanizes your business, allowing customers to connect with your story, values, and team. Your brand can be differentiated from your competitors if you build trust through it.

11. Personalized Photos of the Team and Service Vehicles

- **Why It Matters:** Personal photos create a sense of familiarity and trust. Customers feel more comfortable knowing the faces behind the services they are hiring.

12. Contact Page

- **Why it Matters:** An effective contact page should contain all the necessary information for potential customers to reach out, such as phone numbers, email addresses, and a contact form.

13. Privacy Policy and Terms of Service Page

- **Why It Matters:** These pages are essential for legal compliance and building trust. They show that you are a legitimate business that respects customer privacy and operates transparently.

14. Service Area Page with a Map

- **Why It Matters:** A service area page with a map helps customers quickly determine if you cover their location. It improves user experience and local SEO.

15. Unique Content

- **Why It Matters:** Unique and original content sets your website apart from competitors and enhances your SEO efforts. High-quality content that addresses common customer questions and provides valuable information can position you as an industry expert and drive more traffic to your site.

It will be easier to attract and convert leads if you incorporate these elements into your website. As the first point of contact between you and potential clients, ensure your website leaves a positive impression.

Importance of Mobile Responsiveness

What is Mobile Responsiveness?

Mobile responsive websites can adapt their layout and functionality to various screen sizes, particularly smartphones and tablets. Whenever users access a mobile-friendly website, they experience a seamless and enjoyable experience, regardless of how they access it. Elements such as text, images, and navigation must be adapted to make the site easier to read and usable on smaller screens.

Why Mobile Responsiveness is So Important

It is imperative that home service companies have a mobile-friendly website. It is becoming increasingly important for businesses to design a mobile experience that caters to homeowners looking for services on their mobile devices. Mobile responsiveness is illustrated by these key statistics:

- **54% of All Web Traffic**: As of Q4 2023, 54% of all web traffic came through mobile phones (Statista). This means that more than half of your potential customers are likely accessing your website from a mobile device.

- **First Impressions Matter:** Users form an opinion about a website in just 0.05 seconds. A mobile-friendly design helps make a positive first impression, encouraging users to stay and explore.

- **North American Trends:** 45% of web traffic in North America comes from mobile devices (Statista). This indicates a strong preference for mobile browsing in your target market.

- **User Expectations:** 61% of users say they'll go to another site if they don't find what they're looking for within about five seconds. A mobile-responsive website ensures that users can quickly and easily find the necessary information.

- **Return Visits:** 74% of online users will return to a mobile-friendly website. This backs up the importance of optimizing your site for mobile to encourage repeat visitors.

- **Speed Matters:** 73% of users have encountered a mobile website that loaded too slowly. Websites should load within three seconds. Providing a positive user experience is as important as providing fast loading times.

A mobile-responsive website is more than just a nice-to-have for a home service business to succeed. A consistent and positive user experience is ensured by ensuring your website performs well across all devices. This, in turn, empowers you to attract more leads, improve customer satisfaction, and ultimately grow your business.

User Experience and Conversion Optimization

A home service company's website's user experience (UX) and conversion optimization are not just buzzwords, but powerful tools. It is possible to attract leads to your website and convert them into loyal customers, which will allow your business to grow and thrive.

The Importance of User Experience

Basically, user experience is how your website interacts with your users and how easy it is to navigate and find what they're looking for. The UX of your website can make a big difference in your conversion rates.

- **Simple Navigation:** Your menu structure should be easy to navigate and have a logical structure. Users should be able to find what they need quickly.

- **Fast Loading Times:** As mentioned earlier, users expect websites to load quickly. A slow page can cause a high bounce rate and a loss of leads due to a poor user experience.

- **Readable and Engaging Content:** Content should be easy to read, well-organized, and engaging. It is important to break up text and make it more digestible using headings, bullet points, and images.

- **Mobile-Friendliness:** As I mentioned before, make sure your website is entirely responsive and provides a seamless experience on all devices, specifically mobile phones and tablets.

Conversion Rate Optimization

Conversion rate optimization involves designing your web pages to encourage your website and visitors to take action, like calling your business or scheduling a service. Here are some optimization strategies to improve your website's conversion rates:

- **Clear Call-to-Actions (CTAs):** Every page should have a clear and compelling call-to-action. CTAs should stand out visually and use action-oriented language, such as "Schedule a Service," "Get a Free Quote," or "Call Us Now."

- **Simplified Forms:** Keep contact forms short and easy to fill out. Only ask for the information you absolutely need in order to increase the likelihood of completion.

- **Trust Signals:** Incorporate trust signals such as customer reviews, testimonials, and industry certifications. Using trust logos from associations and displaying award logos are also great for building trust with potential customers.

- **Live Chat:** Implementing a live chat feature can provide immediate assistance to visitors, answer their questions, and guide them toward taking action. Just be careful because if you don't have a CSR monitoring these and replying quickly, it can have the opposite effect on your business.

- **Visual Appeal:** Use high-quality images and a clean, professional design to create a visually appealing website. A well-designed website can enhance trust and encourage users to explore further.

Measuring Success

Remember, it's not enough to implement user experience and conversion optimization strategies. Remember to track KPI metrics and make decisions based on real data to ensure their effectiveness. By monitoring and evaluating metrics like your bounce rate, session duration, and conversion rates, you'll be able to identify areas for improvement and continuously optimize your website. A well-designed website focusing on user experience and conversion optimization will attract visitors and convert them into loyal customers, ultimately leading to more success and growth for your home service company.

Mastering Website Optimization for Search Engines

There is more to online business than having a great-looking website with a great user experience and conversion optimization. The key to thriving online is getting your website discovered by your target audience, and that's where search engine optimization (SEO) comes in.

It's all about using SEO tactics and best practices to get your website found in search engines like Google. SEO can help you get more leads and grow your business by bringing organic (non-paid) traffic to your site. Since most customers will search for services in their area, getting visibility in local search results is especially important for home service companies.

Throughout this section, we'll cover the key SEO elements that every well-optimized home service company site should have. We'll discuss the basics of how search engines work so you can understand why it's important. Whether you're looking to optimize your website's existing on-page

SEO or build an entirely new website, you'll learn what it takes to have a well-optimized website for search engines.

Rest assured, the practices we'll discuss in this section are tried and tested, and they work. Our goal is to equip you with a solid grasp of the foundational SEO practices that will boost your website's visibility, attract more organic traffic, and amplify your digital marketing efforts. These are the ways to optimize your home service business's website for search engines and secure more business with effective SEO.

What is SEO Visibility?

SEO Visibility refers to the likelihood that people will find and click on your website when they search for particular keywords. In simpler terms, it measures how visible your website is in organic search engine results. It generally means that your website ranks higher in search results for those keywords if it has a higher SEO visibility score.

How SEO Visibility is Measured

Most SEO tools measure SEO visibility using similar approaches, but there is no universal method:

1. **Keyword Selection:** First, relevant keywords are chosen based on your website's target audience and goals. You want your website to rank for these keywords in search results.

2. **Ranking Tracking:** The tool then tracks your website's ranking positions for these keywords in search engine results pages (SERPs). The higher you rank, the more visible you are.

3. **Estimating Click-Through Rates (CTR):** Tools often estimate CTRs for keywords based on their ranking position. Greater rankings generally mean higher CTRs.

4. **Keyword Search Volume:** Every keyword's search volume is considered. Keywords with a high search volume have a greater impact on the overall visibility score.

5. **Calculation:** The tool combines all this data to generate a single SEO visibility score, often expressed as a percentage or an index value. This score represents your overall visibility across the selected keywords.

Important Considerations:

- **Relative Metric:** SEO visibility is a relative metric. It's more helpful for tracking your website's performance over time and comparing it to competitors than defining an absolute value.

- **Tool Variations:** Different SEO tools may use slightly different methods for calculating SEO visibility, leading to some score variations.

- **Correlation with Traffic:** A higher SEO visibility score usually correlates with more organic traffic. However, it's not a direct traffic measurement. Other factors, like the quality of your content and user intent, also attract visitors to your website.

How Search Engine Ranking Algorithms Work

There are complex formulas that determine how web pages appear in search results. These algorithms account for hundreds of factors, but the underlying principles include crawling, indexing, and ranking.

1. **Crawling:** Search engines use automated bots, known as crawlers, to navigate web pages and gather information. Crawlers follow hyperlinks from one web page to another, gathering data about content and structure.

2. **Indexing:** The information gathered during crawling is stored in an index, which contains information about the words on each page, the links between pages, and other relevant information.

   Note: Just because a page has been crawled does not mean it will get indexed.

3. **Ranking:** When a user enters a search query, the search engine's algorithm analyzes the index to identify pages relevant to the query. The algorithm then ranks these pages based on various factors, including:

- Relevance: How well the content on a page matches the user's query. This is determined by analyzing the words on the page, the context in which they are used, and other factors.

- Website authority: Trustworthiness and expertise perceived by users and search engine algorithms. This is often measured by the number and quality of links from other websites.

- User experience: How easy the site navigation is to browse and use a website. The appearance of intrusive ads, page loading speed, and mobile-friendliness are all factors to consider.

- Location and Other Factors: Search engines may also consider the user's location, search history, and device type.

There are differences between search engines and queries when it comes to how specific factors are prioritized and how they are ranked. But that's what matters most, making your search experience as useful and relevant as possible.

The factors influencing ranking can change over time because search engine algorithms change. To improve search results and combat spam, search engines continuously update their algorithms. That means the factors influencing rankings can change over time as well.

To fight spam, search engines regularly update their algorithms.

Here are some resources you can check out if you want to learn more about how search engine ranking algorithms work:

- How Google Search Works:

- https://www.google.com/search/howsearchworks/

- A Guide to Google Search Ranking Systems: https://developers.google.com/search/docs/appearance/ranking-systems-guide

You can find in-depth information about how search engines improve the search experience and the factors influencing ranking in these resources.

Topic Silos and Navigation Structure

SEO depends a lot on how your website is structured. When your content is organized into topic silos, it creates a logical flow of information. Defining your topics and navigation can make your website more visible on search engines and better for users.

Understanding Topic Silos

A topic silo method organizes your content by themes or topics so that search engines can understand it more easily. It also makes it easier for visitors to find what they need.

A good website is like a well-organized library with different sections (or silos) for different topics. For example, a plumbing company might have several sections (or silos) such as "Services," "Service Areas," and "About Us."

Why Proper Planning Matters

By planning your site's structure properly, search engines and people can find what they need. For search engines, a clear structure helps with crawling and indexing, which can improve your rankings. For users, an intuitive navigation structure enhances the overall experience, reducing bounce rates and increasing the likelihood of conversions.

Example: Main Menu for a Plumbing Company

The following is an example of how a topic silo structure would be used by a Dallas-based plumbing company.

- **Home**
- **Services**
  - Emergency Plumbing
  - Leak Detection
  - Drain Cleaning
  - Water Heater Repair
  - Sewer Line Repair
- **Service Areas**
  - Dallas
  - Fort Worth
  - Arlington
  - Plano
  - Irving
- **About Us**
  - Our Story
  - Meet the Team

- ○ Testimonials

- **Blog**

  - ○ Plumbing Tips

  - ○ Maintenance Advice

  - ○ Industry News

- **Contact**

Service Silo

All your service-related pages fall under the "Services" silo" This section includes detailed pages for each of your services, such as "Emergency Plumbing," "Leak Detection," etc. For search engines to easily crawl these pages, they need to be interlinked.

Service Area Silo

Similarly, your "Service Areas"' silo contains "pages dedicated to each location you serve. For example, you would have separate pages for "Dallas," "Fort" Worth," "Arlington," and "Irving." Each page should highlight the services you offer in that area and include local SEO elements to target local searches.

Benefits for SEO

When you organize your content into silos, search engines can figure out what's going on between pages, making it easier for you to target specific keywords. For example, a page in the "Dallas" service" section can be optimized for keywords like "Dallas plumbing" services," helping your site rank better.

For SEO and user experience, you've got to think about topic silos when building your website. If your site is easy to navigate, search engines can index your content better, and you rank higher for relevant searches, it's a win-win. In Dallas, this means more visibility, traffic, and customers for plumbing companies.

Why Headings Matter for SEO

Headings are the foundation of any well-structured piece of online content. They lead search engines and humans through your page. Think of them as a table of contents.

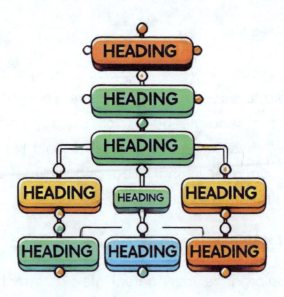

What Makes Headings Important

1. Google uses headings heavily to understand your content's hierarchy and key topics. Properly using headings can boost your page's visibility in search results.

2. Your content breaks down into digestible chunks so readers can quickly scan and find the info they want. This enhances their overall experience and keeps them coming back.

Crafting an Effective Heading Structure

You will need to follow a logical hierarchy that mirrors a traditional document outline:

- **H1**: Your Main Headline

    - This is the title of your page and should be used only once. Make it compelling and keyword-rich.

    - Example: "Emergency Plumbing Services in Dallas"

- **H2**: Section Headings

    - These divide your content into major sections.

    - Examples: "What is Emergency Plumbing?", "Why Choose Us?", "How to Contact Us"

- **H3**: Subsection Headings

- Break down your H2 sections.

- Examples: Under "Why Choose Us?": "Fast Response Time," "Experienced Plumbers," "Affordable Rates"

- **H4-H6**: (Optional) For Deeper Detail

  - Use these sparingly for additional sub-levels if needed.

  - Example: Under "Fast Response Time": "24/7 Availability," "Quick Arrival"

Putting it Together: A Sample Structure

H1: Emergency Plumbing Services in Dallas

H2: What is Emergency Plumbing? (Content explaining...)

H2: Why Choose Our Emergency Plumbing Services?

H3: Fast Response Time (24/7 Availability, Quick Arrival)

H3: Experienced Plumbers (Details about your expertise)

H3: Affordable Rates (Transparent pricing information)

H2: How to Contact Us for Emergency Plumbing (Phone, online form, etc.)

You can make your content search engine-friendly and user-friendly by following this structure. When your headings are well placed, you can push your content to the top of search engines. Your headings are more than just a formatting tool; they are a key strategy that impacts your search engine optimization and user engagement.

Creating Content That Matters

Every page on your website needs unique content, and it's more than just about looking fancy. Unique content is like a superpower for your website, boosting search rankings, offering real value to visitors, and helping you stand out from the crowd.

Why Unique Content Is a Game-Changer

Search engines are like treasure hunters, always searching for fresh and original stuff. When each page on your site has unique content, search engines can easily figure out what your page is all about and how it differs from other pages. This means higher rankings and more people finding your site when they search for specific information.

How Many Words Are Enough?

It sounds surprising, but the number of words on your page can affect your search ranking. Suppose you check out the top results for a popular keyword. In that case, you'll probably notice those pages have a decent amount of content. Your pages should aim for at least the same word count as the top performers to stay competitive. More content means more chances to sprinkle in those important keywords and provide valuable information to your audience.

Using AI Tools Like a Pro

AI tools can be super helpful for sparking ideas and getting your content organized. They're like having a creative assistant who can brainstorm topics, outline your pages, and suggest keywords. However, only let AI do some of the heavy lifting. Your voice, insights, and experiences make your content truly unique and interesting to your audience.

Think of AI tools like a kitchen gadget: they can chop veggies and whip up a sauce, but you're the chef who adds the secret ingredient and brings the whole dish to life. Always review and personalize any content you get from AI so it sounds like you and not a robot.

PRO TIP: Never just copy and paste AI written content into your website without editing and modifying it first. Doing so will harm your rankings and the content will most likely not be indexed by Google.

The Bottom Line

Focus on crafting original, well-written content for every page on your website. Ensure each page has enough content to hold its own against the top search results and use AI tools as a helpful sidekick, not a ghostwriter. This winning combo will help your website climb those search rankings and deliver a better experience for everyone who visits.

SEO FOR HOME SERVICE COMPANIES

Welcome to Chapter 3, where we go deeper into SEO for home service companies like yours. I'm excited to share some of the most impactful strategies that can really move the needle for your online presence. As someone who has spent over 20 years in digital marketing and SEO, I've seen firsthand what works and what doesn't. This chapter will focus on three core categories: On-Page SEO, Off-Page SEO, and Local SEO. These areas are vital for a home service business to be found online and drive more customers to your services. Let's get started and unlock the potential of SEO for your home service business!

On-Page SEO: Best Practices

The objective of on-page SEO is to increase visibility of your web pages in search engines, not just look good. We're going to talk about how to make each page rank higher when people search for your services.

Keywords: The Secret Sauce

When people search for something, they type words into search engines. If you're a plumber, those keywords might be "clogged drain repair" or "local plumbers near me." Think like your customers: what would they type in?

But wait, there's more! Entities are like keywords on steroids. They're super specific terms that help Google understand exactly what your page is about. So, instead of just "plumber," you might use "24-hour emergency plumber in Dallas."

Matching Search Intent

Imagine someone searching for "how to unclog a toilet." They want a helpful guide, not a sales pitch. Your content needs to match what people are actually looking for. That's called search intent. When your content nails it, Google rewards you with higher rankings.

Page Titles and Meta Descriptions: Your Website's Storefront

Think of your page title as the big sign outside your store. It should clearly tell people what the page is about and include your main keyword.

Your meta description is like a catchy slogan underneath. It doesn't directly boost your rankings but makes people want to click on your link in the search results.

Header Tags: Organizing the Chaos

Headers (H1, H2, H3, etc.) are like the chapter titles in a book. They help organize your page and tell Google which parts are most important. Each page should have one H1 summarizing the main topic, with H2 and H3 tags for subtopics. This makes your page easy to read for both people and search engines.

Write for People, Not Robots

Google loves helpful, interesting content that keeps people engaged. Write like you're talking to a friend, not a computer. Show off your expertise, share your knowledge, and be trustworthy. Remember, Google pays attention to E-E-A-T (Experience, Expertise, Authoritativeness, and Trustworthiness) –so be the expert you are!

Images: More Than Just Pretty Pictures

Adding images to your site is not only fun, but it can also benefit your SEO. Give your images descriptive file names (like "clogged-drain-repair.jpg") and alt text (a brief description of the image) so Google knows what it is about.

Make sure you use high-quality images. Don't use images of a sink torn apart, a disassembled dryer, or pieces of a furnace spread all over a basement floor. Nobody wants to see that! Use authentic images of you and your team. It's ok to show a team member in action, make sure it's a nicer photo.

> **PRO TIP:** Try to avoid the over used "blue overalls guy" stock images. You know the ones I'm talking about. :-)

Internal Linking: Connecting the Dots

Internal links are like road signs on your website. They help people (and Google) navigate around. Link between related pages on your site to keep people exploring and to show Google how your content fits together.

Core Web Vitals: The Need for Speed

Your Core Web Vitals are how fast your site loads and how easy it is to use. A slow or glitchy site will hurt your business. Google's PageSpeed Insights tool provides mobile and desktop performance data and recommendations for improvement.

Structured Data: Speaking Google's Language

Structured data is a special code that gives Google more information about your pages. It can help you get fancy search results with extra details (like customer ratings or service areas). This can make your listing stand out and get more clicks.

URLs: Keeping it Simple

Your page's URL is its web address. Keep it short, sweet, and easy to read. A URL like "yourwebsite.com/services/drain-cleaning" is much better than "yourwebsite.com/service123?category=4&id=5678."

By following these on-page SEO tips, you'll be well on your way to getting your home service business noticed online!

Off-Page SEO: Building Authority

Off-page SEO is like word-of-mouth marketing on steroids. It's about building your online reputation and making your business the talk of the town (or at least your service area). For plumbers, electricians, appliance repair pros, and other home service heroes, this is key to attracting more customers and dominating local search results.

Backlinks: Your Digital Votes of Confidence

Think of backlinks as digital recommendations. When reputable websites link to yours, it tells Google you're a trustworthy source. Here's where to focus your efforts:

- Niche Directories: Get listed on directories specific to your industry (e.g., "Best Plumbers in Dallas"). These sites are magnets for potential customers.

- Local News and Blogs: Score a mention in a local news article or guest post on a community blog. This is a fantastic way to build local credibility.

- Partner with Suppliers/Distributors: If you work with specific brands, see if they have partner programs that include backlinks.

- HARO (Help a Reporter Out): Respond to media inquiries relevant to your expertise. This can land you high-quality backlinks from news outlets.

Community Engagement: More Than Just Good Karma

Get involved in your local community! Sponsor a youth sports team, participate in charity events, or collaborate with other businesses. When you're active, people notice, and those mentions often come with backlinks. Plus, it's just a good thing to do!

Online Reviews: Your Digital Reputation

Online reviews are the modern-day word-of-mouth. Encourage your customers to leave 5-star reviews on Google, Yelp, and Facebook. Respond to all reviews (even negative ones) promptly and professionally. A stellar online reputation is like gold for local SEO.

Social Media: Your Virtual Storefront

The more active you are, the more visible you become. Share helpful tips, showcase your work, and run contests. Social media isn't just for cat videos. It's a powerful tool for directly connecting with potential customers. Every interaction can lead to visits to your website.

Content Marketing: Be the Expert

By creating informational content, you can answer customers' questions and solve their problems by writing how-to guides, blog posts about home maintenance, or short videos. Share your content on social media and other platforms to be seen as an authority in your field.

Local Influencers: Team Up for Success

Partner with local influencers who have a strong following in your area. It could be a popular home improvement blogger or a local news personality. They can help spread the word about your business and drive traffic to your website.

Local Citations: NAP Consistency is Key

Name, Address, and Phone Number are the three components of the NAP acronym. Confirm your business details are consistent across all online directory platforms (Google Business Profile, Yelp, Facebook, Chamber of Commerce, and other local business directories). Any discrepancies can confuse Google and hurt your local rankings.

Google Business Profile: Your Local SEO Hub

Your Google Business Profile listing is your home base for local SEO. Keep it updated with accurate information, photos, and regular posts. Encourage reviews, respond to questions, and use the Q&A feature to showcase your expertise.

By consistently working on your off-page SEO, you'll build a trustworthy digital presence that attracts leads, boosts your reputation, and keeps your home service business thriving in the digital age.

Local SEO: Dominating Your Service Area

Local SEO is your digital welcome mat, inviting customers into your service area. If you're an electrician, HVAC pro, appliance repair guru, or any other home service provider, local SEO is the key to getting found online by the people who need you most – your neighbors!

Local vs. National SEO: Apples and Oranges

Consider local SEO targeting folks searching for "emergency plumber near me" or "best HVAC repair in Dallas." It's all about appearing in those search results when potential customers are ready to hire. On the other hand, National SEO is more about casting a wider net, attracting customers across the country with broader search terms.

Your Local SEO Game Plan

Ready to rule the local search results? Here's how:

1. **Google Business Profile (GBP): Your Digital Storefront**

   We'll discuss this more in-depth in a later chapter, but here are some highlights that matter most with your Google Business Profile.

   - **Complete and Accurate**: Make sure your business name, address, phone number, website, hours, and service area are 100% correct.

- **Categories Matter**: Choose the most relevant categories for your business. Don't just pick "plumber." Get specific (e.g., "drain cleaning," "water heater repair").

- **Photos and Videos**: Showcase your best work with high-quality images and videos. Before-and-after shots are always a hit!

- **Reviews**: Your Digital Word-of-Mouth: Encourage happy customers to leave reviews. Respond to all feedback promptly and professionally – good or bad.

- **Q&A**: Answer customer questions directly in the Q&A section of your GBP. This shows you're engaged and knowledgeable.

2. **Local Schema Markup: Speaking Google's Language**

   a. Think of schema as little clues you give Google to understand your website better. Use local business schema to highlight your business name, address, phone number, services, and even customer reviews. This helps you snag those coveted rich snippets in search results.

b. Use service schema across your other pages that are related to your services.

3. Hyperlocal Content: Show Your Local Love

a. Keywords: Sprinkle location-specific keywords throughout your website copy. Think "Dallas AC repair" or "Chicago electrician."

b. Blog Posts: Write about local events, news, or home maintenance tips tailored to your area's climate or common issues.

4. Proximity Matters: Get Found Nearby

a. Your chances of appearing in local searches for specific areas are higher if you have multiple locations. Create separate GBPs for each location.

b. If you're a service-area business (no physical storefront), set your service area in your GBP. This ensures you appear in searches when people nearby are looking for your services.

5. Local Citations: The More, the Merrier

a. You can use citations to display your business name, address, and phone number on other websites. Think of them as digital breadcrumbs leading search engines to your site. Include your business in local directories, industry-specific websites, and social media sites.

6. Online Reviews: Your Reputation Fuel

    a. Reviews aren't just for restaurants. They're crucial for home service businesses too. Ask happy customers for reviews and respond to all feedback, showing you care.

The right local SEO strategies will put your home service business in front of the right people at the right time when they need your expertise. Start applying these strategies today to help your business become the go-to choice in your area. The right local SEO strategies will put your home service business in front of the right people at the right time when they need your expertise. Start applying these strategies today to help your business become the go-to choice in your area.

CHAPTER 4

CONTENT MARKETING

While we covered a lot about SEO in the last chapter, this one is about creating and leveraging content to boost your home service business's online presence. Content marketing is a game-changer because it helps you rank higher on search engines, engages your audience, and turns visitors into customers. In this chapter, we'll laser-focus on three core strategies: Creating Valuable Content, Blogging for SEO and Engagement, and Leveraging Video

Content. Mastering these strategies will increase your visibility, attract targeted traffic, and build lasting customer relationships. Let's get started and unlock the full potential of content marketing for your business!

Creating Valuable Content

What is Valuable Content?

Valuable content is content that genuinely helps your target audience. It's not just about filling pages with words; it's about providing useful, relevant, and engaging information that meets the needs of your readers. For home service businesses, this means creating content that addresses your potential customers' specific concerns and interests.

Characteristics of Valuable Content

1. **Findable:** Your content should be easy to discover. This involves using clear titles, headings, and descriptions that align with what people are searching for.

2. **Readable:** Make sure your content is easy to read. Use a conversational tone, short paragraphs, and bullet points where appropriate. Content can also be digested more easily when accompanied by tables, charts, images, or infographics.

3. **Understandable:** Your audience should easily grasp the information. Avoid jargon and explain concepts clearly. Tailor the complexity of your content to your audience's level of understanding.

4. **Actionable:** Good content often encourages the reader to take some action, whether it's to call for a service, download a guide, or share the information. Clear calls to action (CTAs) are essential.

5. **Sharable:** Make sharing easy with social sharing buttons and prompts. You will reach more readers and attract new customers if your content resonates with them.

How to Create Valuable Content for Home Service Businesses

1. **Understand Your Audience:** Create content that directly addresses the needs of your audience by understanding who they are and what problems they face.

2. **Provide Solutions and Advice:** Write blog posts, how-to guides, and tips for common customer issues. For instance, a plumbing company could create content on "How to Fix a Leaky Faucet" or "Preventing Frozen Pipes in Winter."

3. **Use Real-Life Examples:** Share case studies or testimonials highlighting how your services have

helped other customers. This builds trust and shows the practical application of your services.

4. **Keep it Engaging:** Use stories, visuals, and a friendly tone to engage your audience. Your content must be relatable and interesting to keep people on your page and absorbing the information. Leverage your past experiences and encounters.

5. **Consistency Is Key:** Post consistently so your audience stays engaged and search engines see regular fresh content. Consistency is one of the most challenging things in content marketing. Most business owners do short bursts of content marketing and then stop for long periods before starting back up. It's better to outsource writing tasks that can be consistently done, and you can always tweak and do a quality check on the written content.

Blogging for SEO and Engagement

Before you start writing blog posts, thinking and planning is crucial. Effective blogging for SEO and engagement begins with thorough research and strategic planning. Here's how to get started:

Keyword Research

With keyword research tools, you can identify keywords your potential customers are searching for. Search for long-tail keywords related to what you do and where you are, like "emergency plumbing Dallas."

Here is a list of free tools you can use for keyword research:

- Keyword Generator

- Answer The Public

- Ahrefs Webmaster Tools

- Google Keyword Planner

- Google Search Console

- Google Trends

- SERP Checker

- Keyword Difficulty Checker

- ChatGPT

- Google Gemini

Building an Outline for the Article

A logical outline helps you structure your content and organize your thoughts. Outlines usually include an introduction, key points, subheadings, and conclusions. This keeps your writing focused and makes it easier for readers to follow.

Supporting Content for Service Pages

Blog posts can support your main service pages by providing detailed information on specific topics. For example, a blog post about "How to Unclog a Drain" can link to your drain cleaning service page, enhancing user experience and SEO.

Connecting with Your Audience

Use your blog to let your audience get to know you. Share stories about your team, highlight customer testimonials, and discuss your company's values. Personal content helps build trust and relatability.

Types of Content to Write

- **How-To Guides:** Provide step-by-step instructions on common issues.

- **Listicles:** Create lists such as "Top 10 Plumbing Tips."

- **Checklists and Cheat Sheets:** Offer downloadable resources that are helpful for your audience.

- **Case Studies:** Showcase your successful projects to demonstrate your expertise.

These strategies will help you create engaging, SEO-friendly blog posts that will gain the attention of your target audience and keep them engaged.

Leveraging Video Content

Business owners, especially those in the home service field, can benefit from video marketing as a powerful tool that can help propel their companies to new levels of success. It's the art of using videos to connect with your audience, share your expertise, and ultimately drive more customers to your services, promising a brighter future for your company.

Consider an appliance repair company that creates short, engaging videos. These videos could demonstrate how to troubleshoot common refrigerator issues or showcase their technicians' skills in a time-lapse repair video. Such content establishes the company's expertise and resonates with potential customers facing similar problems.

Video content is a great way to increase reach and engagement in your content marketing strategy. It is a great tool for home service companies to showcase their work, connect with customers, and prove how valuable they are. Whether it's DIY repair videos or fun behind-the-scenes peeks at your company's culture, videos can grab your audience's attention and convert them. Videos can give your customers an insider's view of your company, allowing them to learn more about you.

Why Video Marketing is Powerful for Home Service Companies

Video marketing is effective because it engages multiple senses, increasing the impact and memory of your content. Video can effectively show your expertise, demonstrate your services, and connect with your audience. For home service companies, they are particularly useful since they are capable of demonstrating the quality of your work and visually explaining complex issues.

Tips for Engaging Customers with Informative and Entertaining Content

Creating engaging video content for your home service business is essential for building trust and capturing the attention of potential customers. Here are some tips to help you make the most of your videos:

- **Appearance is Important:** First impressions matter. Wear a clean uniform and ensure the background is tidy and professional. This helps present a polished and trustworthy image to your audience.

- **Keep it Short and Sweet:** Attention spans are short, so aim for concise, informative videos. Keep your videos concise, focusing on delivering valuable information quickly and clearly.

- **Show Your Personality:** Let your company's culture and values shine through. Whether a friendly greeting or a humorous touch, showing your personality helps build a connection with your viewers and makes your content more relatable.

- **Use High-Quality Visuals and Clear Audio:** Good production quality enhances credibility. Ensure your videos have clear audio and high-quality visuals. Use good lighting, a stable camera, and a quiet environment to avoid distractions and make your content more professional.

Following these tips can strengthen your brand's online presence by creating engaging, informative, and entertaining video content.

Incorporating Related Videos in Your Blog Posts

Embedding relevant videos in your blog posts can enrich the content and keep visitors engaged longer. For instance, a blog post about "Common Dishwasher Problems" could include a video demonstration of troubleshooting tips.

Turning Your Blog Posts into Video Content

Repurposing your written content into videos is a straightforward and practical way to enhance your marketing strategy. For example, a 'How to Properly

Maintain Your Dishwasher' blog post can be turned into a step-by-step video tutorial. This approach saves time and appeals to different audiences, giving you the confidence to expand your reach.

The Best Places to Post Your Videos

Engage your audience where they are most likely to be:

- **YouTube:** The second most searched website worldwide is YouTube, right after Google. Homeowners often turn to YouTube for quick fixes before calling a professional. Your appliance repair company can tap into this vast audience by creating high-quality, informative videos that address common problems. This platform is excellent for reach and discoverability, allowing potential customers to find your content easily and see your expertise in action. Engaging video content on YouTube can attract more viewers, drive traffic to your website, and convert viewers into customers.

- **Facebook and Instagram:** Facebook and Instagram are ideal platforms for video content because they facilitate high engagement and sharing. On Facebook, videos can be shared easily among users, leading to greater reach and visibility. With its Stories and IGTV features, Instagram allows for creative and dynamic video presentations. Both platforms support live videos, which can be used for real-time engagement with your audience, answering questions, and showcasing your services. Your local community will appreciate the interactive and shareable content you can create with these social media channels.

- **TikTok:** TikTok is a great way to show off your skills and personality. Create quick tips, before-and-afters, or behind-the-scenes videos. People who like similar content can learn about your videos through the TikTok algorithm, making it a great way to see your videos.

- **Your Website:** Embedding videos on your website's relevant service pages and blog posts can significantly enhance user experience. When a visitor lands on a service page like "Water Heater Repair," a step-by-step repair process video can provide valuable insights and visually demonstrate your expertise. Videos can also break up text in blog posts and make them more engaging. This multimedia approach not only helps to retain visitors longer but also boosts your site's credibility and can improve SEO by reducing bounce rates and increasing time spent on your site.

Don't Worry About Making Perfect Videos

Your videos don't need to be flawless. Authenticity often resonates more with viewers than polished perfection. When you focus on delivering valuable information, your audience will appreciate the effort and sincerity. Minor imperfections, like a stumble over words or an unpolished background, can make your videos more genuine and relatable. Viewers are more interested in your helpful content than in cinematic quality, relieving you of the pressure to be a professional videographer.

In the long run, you will develop a stronger relationship with your audience by delivering engaging video content. A genuine video can foster trust and make your business more approachable. Don't stress over every detail; provide clear, useful, and engaging videos that addresses your audience's needs without stressing over every detail.

5

SOCIAL MEDIA MARKETING

There's more to social media than staying in touch with family and friends. They're powerful tools for growing your business too. By leveraging social media effectively, you can drive more leads and conversions, boost your visibility, and engage your audience. In this chapter, we'll talk about how to get your business on social media. Whether you are on Facebook, X, Instagram, TikTok, or LinkedIn, the real goal of a solid social media presence is to generate leads and sales for your business.

The power of social media lies in its ability to reach potential customers, build brand awareness, and drive engagement. So, having a strong social media presence isn't just optional; it's essential. Here's why:

- **Increased Visibility**: Marketing your services on social media allows you to reach new customers you didn't know existed.

- **Customer Engagement:** Interacting with your customers via social media lets you answer their questions, address their concerns, and build a community around your business. It would be best to build trust and loyalty to build repeat business and referrals with your audience.

- **Cost-Effective Marketing:** Social media marketing is usually more inexpensive than traditional advertising. Many platforms offer free tools to create and manage business profiles, and paid advertising options are available at various budget levels.

- **Real-Time Feedback:** Social media provides instant feedback from your audience. Analyzing your content can help you target your audience more effectively.

- **SEO Benefits:** Active social media profiles can boost your search engine rankings. Sharing content, earning likes and shares, and having a presence on multiple platforms can improve your online visibility. Google identifies this activity as "Social Signals" and uses this information to evaluate your online business presence.

Overview of Popular Social Media Platforms

Social media to connect with customers, showcase expertise, and build trust can be an extremely powerful tool for growing home service businesses. Here's a look at the top platforms and how you can use them effectively:

1. Facebook (3+ Billion Monthly Active Users)

- Best for:
  - Building local community awareness

- Commenting and direct messaging with customers

- Sharing before-and-after photos of completed projects

- Advertise to homeowners in the area where you provide services

- Creating groups for Q&A or sharing tips (e.g., "Appliance Repair Tips for [Your City]")

2. Instagram (2+ Billion Monthly Active Users)

- Best for:

  - Visually showcasing your work (high-quality photos and videos of repairs/installations)

  - Utilizing Instagram Stories to share behind-the-scenes glimpses of your team or quick DIY tips

  - Running contests or promotions to engage your followers

  - Using relevant hashtags to increase visibility (e.g., #appliancerepair, #hvaclife, #plumbersofinstagram)

3. TikTok (1.2+ Billion Monthly Active Users)

- Best for:

  - Creating short, engaging videos that demonstrate your expertise

- Sharing "how-to" content (e.g., "How to Unclog a Sink in 5 Minutes")

- Participating in trending challenges or creating your own to increase brand awareness

4. LinkedIn (875+ Million Members)

- Best for:

  - Establishing yourself as an industry expert by sharing articles or insights

  - Networking with other local businesses and potential partners (e.g., realtors, property managers)

  - Reaching a more professional audience for commercial services

5. X (formerly Twitter) (550+ Million Monthly Active Users)

- Best for:

  - Sharing real-time updates on service disruptions or emergencies

  - Engaging in conversations relevant to your industry

  - Providing quick customer service responses

  - Joining relevant Twitter chats to connect with potential clients

Important Considerations:

- **Choose the right platforms:** Focus your efforts on the social platforms where your target customer is most actively searching for your services.

- **Be consistent:** Post often to keep your audience updated and engaged.

- **High-quality content:** Invest in good photos and videos to showcase your professionalism.

- **Engage with your audience:** Respond to comments, answer questions, and build relationships with your audience.

- **Track your results:** Use available analytics tools to measure your success and adjust your strategy.

By strategically using these platforms, home service businesses can effectively market their services, build a strong online presence, and grow their customer base.

Setting Up Your Social Media Profiles

Setting up your social media profiles correctly, in alignment with your branding, not only enhances your business identity but also boosts your customers' confidence in your services. Integrating them with your website further strengthens your online presence.

Choosing the Right Platforms for Your Business

Before setting up your profiles, consider which platforms best suit your home service business. Since we've already discussed the benefits of each platform, decide where your target audience is most active and where your content will shine the brightest. For a home service business, Facebook, Instagram, TikTok, LinkedIn, and YouTube are often the best choices.

Optimizing Profiles with Consistent Branding and Complete Information

Once you've chosen your platforms, it's time to set up your profiles. Remember, these should be business accounts, not personal ones. Business accounts offer tools and analytics necessary for managing and growing your social media presence. Here's how to optimize them:

1. **Profile and Cover Photos:** Use your business logo as your profile picture. This ensures brand recognition. Make sure your cover photo represents your business and is visually appealing. For example, a collage of your best projects or a professional photo of your team at work.

2. **Username and Handle:** Choose a username consistent across all platforms and easy to remember. Ideally, it should be your business name. This will look better in emails, print materials, and

other marketing efforts, making it easier for customers to find you.

3. **Bio and Description:** Write a clear, concise bio that tells visitors who you are, what you do, and where you do it. Ensure your keywords are relevant to the services your target audience might seek. Make sure to add your location and contact information.

4. **Contact Information:** Keep your contact information accurate and up-to-date. Make sure you include your phone number, email, and physical address. Make it as easy as possible for customers to contact you.

5. **Website Link:** Always include a link to your website in your profile. This drives traffic from your social media to your main site, where customers can learn more about your services and contact you directly.

6. **Call to Action (CTA):** Utilize the call-to-action buttons on platforms like Facebook and Instagram. This could be a "Book Now," "Contact Us," or "Learn More" button that directs users to take immediate action.

7. **Consistent Branding:** Use the same color scheme, tone of voice, and style across all your social media profiles. Keeping your brand consistent builds trust and makes it easier to recognize.

8. **Visual Content:** Regularly update your profiles with high-quality images and videos. Showcase your work, behind-the-scenes looks, and customer testimonials. Your audience will be engaged if you provide them with visual content.

Integrating Social Media with Your Website

Adding links to your social media accounts on your website will maximize their impact. Here's how:

1. **Social Media Icons:** Incorporate social media links prominently on your website using social media icons, ensuring they are easily accessible to visitors.

2. **Share Buttons:** Incorporate social sharing buttons in your blog posts and service pages. As a result, your content and pages can be shared by visitors with their networks, which allows you to reach a larger audience.

3. **Calls to Action:** Use calls to action on your website to motivate visitors to follow you on social media. For example, "Follow us on Facebook for the latest updates and special offers!"

The setup and optimization of your social media profiles, in conjunction with how you integrate them with your website, will enhance your brand visibility and make it easier for your customers to get in touch with you.

Engaging with Your Audience

Engaging with your audience on social media is crucial for building relationships and driving business. It's not just about posting updates; it's about creating meaningful interactions that keep your audience interested and connected to your brand. Here are some practical tips for home service companies to effectively engage with the local community and turn those interactions into service bookings and sales.

Practical Tips for Engagement

1. **Respond to Comments and Messages Promptly**

   If you are tagged in a post, make sure you are promptly responding to their comments and messages. This shows that you are attentive and value their input. Answering questions and addressing concerns can build trust and prompt potential customers to book an appointment.

2. **Share Valuable and Relevant Content**

   Post valuable content to your audience, such as DIY tips, maintenance advice, or seasonal reminders related to your services. For example, an HVAC company could share tips on preparing your home for winter.

3. Use Interactive Content

Create polls, quizzes, and questions to encourage your audience to interact with your posts. For instance, ask followers to vote on the best time of year to schedule a home service.

4. Join Local Facebook Groups and NextDoor

These platforms are excellent for engaging with local homeowners. Participate in discussions, offer helpful advice, and answer questions related to your services. Remember, your posts should not be self-promoting, which is against most group guidelines. If you want to share a special promotion, always obtain permission from the group admins first.

5. Share Community Involvement

Highlight your involvement in community activities, such as speaking at local events, volunteering, or supporting charities. This demonstrates that you are an active and caring community member, which can enhance your reputation and attract more customers.

6. Run Contests and Giveaways

Contests and giveaways can generate excitement and increase engagement. Offer a free service or a discount to the winner. Ensure that the contest rules encourage participants to like, share, and comment on your posts.

7. Feature Your Customer Reviews

Share positive reviews and feedback from your satisfied customers. This builds trust and shows potential customers the quality of your services. Encourage your customers to leave reviews on your social media pages, as these reviews could be displayed on your Google Business Profile.

8. Use Live Videos

Live videos are a great way to interact with your audience in real-time. Host Q&A sessions, show behind-the-scenes of your work, or demonstrate how to solve common issues. Live interactions can make your business more relatable and trustworthy.

9. Highlight Special Promotions and Services

Inform your audience about special promotions, seasonal services, or new offerings. Make sure these posts are engaging and provide clear calls to action, encouraging followers to book a service or contact you for more information.

10. Share User Generated Content

Share pictures and videos of your completed work or your service. Sharing user-generated content will foster community and authenticity and show potential customers what your services are like in real life.

By consistently engaging with your audience in these ways, you can build strong relationships, enhance your brand's reputation, and ultimately drive more service bookings and sales. Remember, social media is about creating a dialogue, so be active, responsive, and genuine in your interactions.

Paid Social Media Campaigns

A paid social media campaign can make a big difference if you want to reach a larger, more targeted audience. Using social media advertising effectively involves creating a creative strategy, selecting the right platforms, and using effective advertising tactics.

Managing Your Social Media Advertising Campaigns

In order to manage your social media advertising campaigns successfully, you need to plan, execute, and monitor them carefully. To help you stay on top of your campaigns, follow these steps:

1. **Set Clear Goals**: Define what you want to achieve with your ads. This could be increasing website traffic, generating leads, or boosting service bookings.

2. **Identify Your Target Audience**: Use the demographic and interest-based targeting features on social media platforms to reach your ideal customers. This might mean targeting homeowners in specific geographic locations for a home service business.

3. **Create a Budget**: Decide how much you will spend on your campaigns. Allocate your budget based on the platforms offering the best investment return.

4. **Analyze Your Ads:** You can analyze their performance using tools like Facebook Ads Manager and Google Analytics. We're talking click-through rates (CTRs), conversion rates, and cost per click (CPCs).

5. **Monitor and Optimize**: Regularly review your ad performance and adjust as needed. This could involve tweaking your ad copy, adjusting your targeting, or reallocating your budget to better-performing ads.

A Creative Social Media Advertising Strategy

A creative advertising strategy can help your home service business stand out and attract more customers. Here are some tips to build an effective strategy:

1. **Craft Compelling Ad Copy**: Write clear, concise, and engaging ad copy highlighting your services'

benefits. Use action-oriented language and include a strong call to action (CTA).

2. **Use Eye-Catching Visuals**: Create images and videos that grab the attention of your target audience. Showcase your work, such as before-and-after photos of home repairs or short video clips of your team in action. Canva.com is an amazing tool for creating visual ad content for your campaigns.

3. **Offer Promotions and Discounts**: Entice potential customers with special offers, discounts, or limited-time deals. Highlight these in your ads to encourage immediate action.

4. **Tell a Story**: Create ads that tell a story about your business. This could be a testimonial from a satisfied customer, a behind-the-scenes look at your operations, or a success story of a particularly challenging job.

5. **Test Different Ad Formats**: Experiment with various ad formats. Using various options such as carousel ads, video ads, and slideshow ads, you can choose the best-performing ad types to optimize further. The ad copy that performs the best might not be the cheapest, but it converts better. Or you might have ads that are cheap but need to convert better. So, never make the cost your primary decision for which ads you want to keep.

Best Social Media Platforms to Advertise On

Choosing the right social media platforms for your ads is crucial. Here are the best platforms for home service businesses:

1. **Facebook**: Ideal for reaching a broad audience. Facebook's advanced targeting options and ad formats make it a top choice for home service businesses.

2. **Instagram**: Great for visual content. Use Instagram to showcase high-quality images and videos of your work.

3. **TikTok**: Perfect for engaging, short-form videos. Create fun and informative content that can go viral and reach a younger audience.

4. **LinkedIn**: Best for B2B marketing. LinkedIn can help you connect with decision-makers and professionals if your services cater to businesses such as property managers or if you provide commercial repairs and installations.

5. **Nextdoor**: Focused on local communities. This platform is excellent for reaching homeowners in your service area and getting local recommendations.

Social Media Advertising Tactics

To get the most out of your social media advertising, use these effective tactics:

1. **Retargeting**: Use retargeting ads to reach people who have already visited your website or interacted with your content. This keeps your business top-of-mind and encourages them to convert.

2. **Lookalike Audiences**: A lookalike audience is a demographic or group similar to your current and past customers. Using lookalike audiences, you can reach similar potential customers who share the same characteristics and needs as your existing customers.

3. **Local Targeting**: Geo-target your ads on specific geographic areas where you offer services. This ensures that your ads are seen by people who are most likely to become your customers, and your ads will not be shown to people outside your service area.

4. **A/B Testing**: Continuously test different versions of your ads to see what works best. Optimize your campaigns by experimenting with headlines, images, ad copy, and CTAs.

5. **Engage with Your Audience**: Respond to comments and messages on your ads. Engaging with potential

customers can build trust and increase their likelihood of choosing your services.

Your home service business can drive real results by implementing these paid social media strategies and tactics.

GOOGLE BUSINESS PROFILE OPTIMIZATION

A well-optimized Google Business Profile (GBP) can make or break the success of a home service business. As the first impression many potential customers will have of your business, your GBP must be fully optimized to attract and convert leads. From setting up and verifying your profile to optimizing for local searches and managing reviews, this chapter will guide you through the essential steps to enhance your online presence and visibility.

A properly optimized GBP improves your chances of appearing in local search results and builds trust and credibility with your audience. Let's dive in and ensure your Google Business Profile works hard for your business.

Setting Up and Verifying Your Profile

A verified Google Business Profile will boost your credibility and improve your chances of appearing in local search results. This will help you find your home service business more easily online. Here's how to set up and verify your profile.

Step 1: Create Your Profile

1. Sign In to Google Business Profile: Go to the Google Business Profile website. You'll need to sign in with your Google account. You'll need to create an account if you don't have one. https://www.google.com/business/

2. Enter Your Business Name: Type in your business name. If it appears in the list of suggestions, select it. If Google does not show it, click "Add your business to Google."

3. Choose Your Business Category: This is the most important step for your GBP. Selecting the proper

category will make or break whether your business listing is displayed to customers looking for your services. Select the category that best matches your business. This helps Google understand your services and connect you with relevant search queries.

4. Add Your Location: In this field, you can specify your service areas instead of your physical location if you deliver services to your customers at their locations. As long as you make in-person contact with customers, your business can have a profile even if you don't have a physical address. In addition, hybrid businesses that serve customers at their business address and visit or deliver directly to customers can create a profile. A service-area business can also have a profile if it visits or delivers directly to customers rather than serving them at its business address, like a plumber or cleaning service.

5. Fill in Contact Information: Ensure your phone number and website URL are included so customers can easily reach you.

6. Finish and Manage: Complete the setup by following the prompts. Once done, you can manage your profile and update information as needed.

Step 2: Verify Your Business

To appear in local search results and on Google Maps, your Google Business Profile must be verified.

Types of Business Profiles

1. **Service-Area Business:** This type of business visits or delivers to customers directly but doesn't serve them at its business address. Examples include plumbers and cleaning services. Listing your service areas by city or postal code would be best.

2. **Hybrid Business:** This business serves customers at its physical location and also visits or delivers to customers. An example would be a restaurant that offers dine-in and delivery services. You can display your address, set business hours for your location, and specify a service area.

3. **Service-Area Specifics:**

   - You can't set your service area as a distance around your business.

   - Specify your service area by city, postal code, or other areas.

   - You can have up to 20 service areas, but the boundaries should be about 2 hours of driving time from your base.

Verification Process

1. **Add or Claim Your Business Profile:**

    -   Go to Google My Business and add or claim your profile. Enter your business details according to the prompts.

2. **Choose a Verification Method:**

    One thing to remember when verifying your Google Business Profile is that some verification methods might not be available depending on your type of business and chosen category. In most cases you'll have to do a phone or video verification method. Google has had to go to these extremes to weed out the lead generation companies that have unfortunately ruined the ease of getting a legitimate listing.

    -   **Postcard Verification:** Using the postcard verification method, Google will send a verification code via postcard to your business address. Input the code in your Google Business Profile account.

    -   **Phone or Email Verification:** If you're eligible, a code will be sent to your phone or email address. You'll need to enter that code into your Google Business Profile.

- **Video Verification:** For some businesses, you might need to create a video showing your business location, equipment, and proof of operation. Upload the video, and Google will review it within a few days.

3. **Prepare for Verification:**

   - Ensure your business name, address, and phone number are exactly the same across all platforms (website, social media).

   - If you've relocated, update your website with the correct address and Google Map schema.

   - Add exterior photos with signage to your Google Profile.

   - Have your business license and a utility bill handy for additional verification.

4. **Complete Verification:**

   - You must follow the instructions for the verification method you selected. This may involve entering a code received via mail, phone, or email or completing a video verification.

   - Google may review your verification, which can take up to 5 business days. You will receive a notification once verified.

5. **Post-Verification Steps:**

   - Your business information may take a few weeks to appear across Google services.

   - You can update and add information to your profile at any time.

6. **Finding Your Profile:**

   - On Google Search, search for "my business" or your business name and city.

   - You can tap your profile picture or initials using the Google Maps app, then "Your Business Profile."

Following these steps, you can successfully set up and verify your Google Business Profile, ensuring potential customers can easily find your home service business online.

Optimizing for Local Searches

Once your business is verified, it's time to optimize your profile to ensure it stands out and attracts potential customers.

1. **Complete All Information:** Ensure all your business details are accurate and complete. This includes your business hours, address, phone number, and website.

2. **Add High-Quality Photos:** Upload high-resolution images of your business, team, and work. Photos make your profile more appealing and can help attract more customers.

3. **Write a Compelling Description:** Craft a concise business description highlighting your services, unique selling points, and what customers can expect.

4. **List Your Services:** Include a detailed list of your services to help potential customers understand what you do and improve your chances of appearing in relevant searches.

You'll get more local customers if you set up and verify your Google Business Profile. Your business will appear in front of people searching for home services in your area, which will help you stand out.

Optimizing for Local Searches

Optimizing your Google Business Profile (GBP) ensures your home service business stands out in local search results. Ensuring your profile is complete, accurate, and engaging increases your chances of attracting local customers searching for your services. Here's a detailed checklist to help you optimize your GBP effectively.

Google Business Profile Optimization Checklist

1. **Optimize Your Business Name:**

    *   Use the exact name of your business as it appears on official documents like your business license. Avoid adding extra keywords or location names to your business name. This keeps your profile professional and compliant with Google's guidelines.

2. **Add Your Business Categories:**

    *   Choose relevant categories that accurately describe your services. For instance, if you run a plumbing business, select categories like "Plumber" or "Emergency Plumbing."

3. Add Your Business Address:

- Ensure your address is precise and complete. If your business serves customers at their locations, check the box indicating that you provide service at your business address. This helps in showing your correct service area to potential customers.

4. Add Your Phone Number:

- Include your business phone number with the area code. This makes it easy for customers to contact you and also helps in local search rankings.

5. Add Your Website:

- If you have a business website, add it to your profile. This gives customers more information about your services and can drive traffic to your site.

6. Add Your Photos and Videos:

- Include high-quality videos and photos of your business, products, and services. Add team photos and images of your service vehicles for additional impact and recognition of your brand.

7. Respond to Reviews:

- You should respond to all reviews, positive or negative. Replying shows you care about customer feedback and your commitment to exceptional customer service. It also encourages more happy customers to leave reviews.

8. Add Your Business Hours:

- Include your regular business hours and any special hours for holidays or events. Accurate hours help customers know when they can reach you.

9. Update Your Information Regularly:

- Keep your business information up-to-date, including hours, phone number, website, and photos. This ensures that customers always have the correct information and can trust your business's reliability.

10. Add Your Business Attributes:

- Use attributes to provide more details about your business, such as whether you accept credit cards, have outdoor seating, or offer Wi-Fi. These small details can make a big difference to potential customers.

11. Use Posts:

- Share updates and promotions with your customers using Google Posts. This feature lets you directly highlight special offers, events, and news on your GBP.

12. Use Google Q&A:

- Answer common questions from customers using the Google Q&A feature. This can save you and your customers time by answering frequently asked questions instantly.

13. Use Google Business Profile Insights:

- Track your business's performance using Google Business Profile Insights. These analytics can help you understand how customers find your profile and their actions, allowing you to make data-driven decisions.

14. Use Keywords in Your Business Description:

- Include relevant keywords in your business description. This helps improve your profile's visibility in search results when customers seek your services.

15. Encourage Customers to Leave Reviews:

- You can increase your Google Business Ranking by inviting satisfied customers to leave a review. Positive reviews not only bring new customers but also improve your search rankings.

16. Monitor Your Google Business Profile:

- Regularly check and manage your Google Business Profile to ensure all information is accurate and up-to-date. Promptly respond to customer reviews and questions.

17. Engage with Your Customers:

- Use your profile to interact with customers by answering questions, responding to reviews, and engaging with your audience. Being proactive and responsive helps build strong relationships and trust with your customers.

By optimizing your Google Business Profile with these steps, you'll attract more customers and enhance your local search visibility. You should regularly update and manage your Google Business Profile to ensure it remains an effective tool for business growth.

Optimizing your Google Business Profile is an ongoing process that requires attention and effort. However, increased visibility, improved customer trust, and higher search rankings make it worth the time. Keep your profile active and engaging, and you'll see a positive impact on your business.

Resource: You can download our **Ultimate Google Business Profile Optimization Checklist for Home Service Companies** at the following URL:

Managing Reviews and Interactions

Managing customer reviews and interactions is important for growing a positive online presence and building trust with potential customers. The way you handle reviews, positive and negative, will affect your company's reputation and search ranking.

Importance of Review Content and Signals

While the content of customer reviews does not directly impact your search rankings, the signals generated by reviews do. Reviews send important geo-location signals to Google, indicating where your customers are when they leave a review. This helps Google better understand the relevance of your business to local searchers.

The manner and speed of your responses also matter. Promptly replying to reviews shows that you are an active business that engages frequently with customers. This can positively influence how your business is perceived both by customers and search engines.

Responding to Positive Reviews

Positive reviews are a great opportunity to show appreciation and build customer loyalty. When responding to positive reviews, mention the customer's name and the specific service or product you provided. This personal touch shows that you value their feedback and remember their service.

Example of a Positive Customer Review:

"ACME Appliance Repair did an amazing job fixing my refrigerator! It stopped cooling, and they were able to come out the same day. The technician was professional, friendly, and explained everything clearly. Highly recommend their service!"

Example of a Good Reply:

*"Thank you, **Mrs. Johnson**, for your kind words! We're thrilled to hear that you were satisfied with our service. Working on your **LG refrigerator** was a pleasure, and we're glad we could resolve the **no-cooling issue** quickly. If you need any assistance in the future, please don't hesitate to contact us!"*

In this example reply, you can see it was very personalized by using the customer's name, the brand of refrigerator they have, and the type of problem that was resolved.

Responding to Negative Reviews

In the event of a negative review, it is important to respond promptly and professionally. This displays your commitment to customer satisfaction and mitigates the impact of the review. You should acknowledge the problem, take responsibility, apologize, and offer a solution. Keep in mind that most issues can be resolved through clear communication.

Example of a Negative Customer Review:

"ACME Appliance Repair was late for the appointment and didn't fix my refrigerator properly. I had to call them back to get it resolved. Very disappointed with their service."

Example of a Good Reply:

*"Hello, **Mrs. Johnson**. We're **very sorry** to hear about your experience and **apologize for any inconvenience** caused. Our goal is to provide timely and effective service, and we regret that **we didn't meet your expectations**. We've reached out to you privately to discuss how we can fix this issue and improve our overall customer service. Thank you for bringing this to our attention."*

In this example reply, you can see all of the elements we discussed previously being used. The customer's name was used, the apology was immediate, and then they took ownership by saying they didn't meet the expectations of the customer. And finally, contact was made to gather further feedback for improvement.

If you are able to turn a negative review into a positive experience for the customer, you can ask them to revise their original review and this is usually even more impactful in the end.

Tips for Managing Reviews and Interactions

1. **Acknowledge Every Review:** Always acknowledge the customer's feedback, whether the review is positive or negative. This shows that you value their opinion and are committed to providing excellent service.

2. **Personalize Your Responses:** Mention the customer's name and specific details about their service. This adds a personal touch and shows that you care about their experience.

3. **Respond Quickly:** Respond to reviews as timely as possible. Timely responses indicate that you are attentive and proactive in addressing customer feedback.

4. **Stay Professional and Courteous:** Even if the review is negative, maintain a professional and courteous tone. Avoid getting defensive or confrontational.

5. **Resolve Negative Reviews:** When reviewing negative reviews, apologize for any issues and

discuss a way to make things right. This can help turn a negative experience into a positive one.

Managing reviews and interactions well will build a good reputation, increase customer trust, and make your business more visible on local search. Reviews show search engines that you care about your customers and show them your business is reliable and active.

7

CRACKING THE GOOGLE ADS CODE

In this chapter, we're going to dive headfirst into the wild world of Google Ads! Now, I know what you might be thinking: "Google Ads? Isn't that just for big companies with massive marketing budgets?" Not at all! In fact, Google Ads can be a goldmine for home service businesses like yours—if you know how to crack the code.

Picture this: you're a local plumber, HVAC technician, or appliance repair guru, and you want more local customers. Google Ads can help you connect with those folks who are frantically Googling "emergency plumber near me" while knee-deep in a flooded basement. But it's not just about throwing money at Google and hoping for the best. Oh no, my friends, there's an art and a science to this game.

I'll start with an introduction to Pay-Per-Click (PPC) advertising, which is the backbone of Google Ads. We'll discuss the strategies and best practices that will make your ads stand out in the sea of search results. And finally, we'll harness the power of Google Local Services Ads to ensure you're the top choice when locals need your services the most.

So grab a cup of coffee and let's get ready to turn those clicks into customers and those ad dollars into gold. It's time to crack the Google Ads code!

Introduction to Pay-Per-Click (PPC)

Alright, folks, let's get down to the nitty-gritty of Google Ads and how it can revolutionize your home service business. Imagine reaching potential customers at the exact moment they're searching for services like yours - appliance repair, plumbing, HVAC, or electrical. Sounds like a dream, right?

Well, that's the magic of Google Ads. But hold on, it's not all sunshine and rainbows. There are some pitfalls to avoid to ensure you're not just throwing money into a digital black hole. Let's break this down using the AIDA model: Attention, Interest, Desire, and Action.

Attention: The Power of Google Ads for Home Services

Google Ads offers an unparalleled opportunity for home service companies to reach potential customers right when they need you most. Picture this: someone's air conditioner breaks down during a scorching summer day in Albuquerque. They hop on Google, type in "AC repair near me," and there you are, front and center with a perfectly timed ad. This kind of visibility can significantly boost your customer acquisition and growth.

Interest: Why Google Ads Works

Targeting Customers with Precision

Google Ads excels at connecting your business with potential customers precisely when they're searching for the services you offer. This precise targeting ensures that your ad appears to potential customers who are actively looking for home services, increasing the likelihood of conversion.

Flexibility to Match Your Needs

Whether you're a small local one-person show or a larger multi-tech operation, Google Ads can be tailored to fit your budget and objectives. This flexibility means you can allocate your marketing dollars efficiently and reach your target audience without breaking the bank.

Measurable Outcomes

With comprehensive analytics and tracking tools like Google Analytics and Google Business Profile insights, you can measure your success with clear ROI tracking. From the number of clicks and conversions to detailed performance analytics, you have all the data you need to optimize your campaigns.

A Range of Ad Formats

Google Ads offers various ad formats to cater to different marketing needs. From text-based search ads to visually engaging display ads, leveraging the right mix can enhance your visibility and engagement with potential customers.

Desire: The Dark Side of Google Ads

Tackling Platform Complexity

Let's face it, Google Ads can be a beast to manage. Its extensive features and options present a steep learning curve. For small business owners, this complexity can be daunting and time-consuming.

Competing in a Crowded Space

The competitive nature of Google Ads, especially for high-demand keywords, can drive up costs. Small businesses often find themselves competing against larger companies with bigger advertising budgets. Managing these costs while maintaining effective ad visibility requires strategic bidding and keyword selection.

Quality Score Challenges

Google's Quality Score is critical to your ad's position and cost-per-click. Factors like ad relevance, landing page quality, and click-through rate impact this score. Improving your Quality Score is essential but can be complex, requiring a strategic approach to ad copy and targeting.

Action: Making Google Ads Work for You

Despite its challenges, Google Ads can be a goldmine if you know how to navigate it. Here are a few steps to get you started:

1. **Start Small and Scale:** Begin with a modest budget to test the waters and understand what works best for your business. Never increase your ad spend budget by large amounts at one time. This could cause a negative effect on your ad performance. It is best to adjust your ad spend incrementally over a period of time so you can more easily monitor and adjust as time goes on.

2. **Use Specific Keywords:** Focus on long-tail keywords that are highly relevant to your services. This helps reduce competition and cost. Don't forget to add negative keywords to your campaign too. Negative keywords will help your ads to not be displayed when someone searches for similar services that you do not offer. For example, an appliance repair company might not service small appliances such as blenders and mixers, or vacuums or televisions. So adding those as negative keywords would not allow your ads to be displayed for those search queries.

3. **Geo-Fence Your Service Area:** One thing that many home service companies miss is geo-fencing your target service area. Make sure your ads are only displayed to people that are searching for your services within your service area.

4. **Optimize Your Ad Copy:** Write compelling ad copy that speaks directly to the needs of your potential customers.Google Ads has built in tools with suggestions that will increase your ad quality score. Not all recommendations are good though, so use your best judgment here.

5. **Monitor and Adjust:** Regularly check your campaign performance and make necessary adjustments to improve results. If you make adjustments, make small changes and then monitor the performance. Making too many changes will make it hard to track

if the changes you made are working in a positive or negative way.

Mastering Google Ads can turn clicks into customers and those ad dollars into real profit. It's time to harness the power of PPC and watch your home service business thrive. So, are you ready to crack the Google Ads code? Let's get started!

Google Ads: Strategies and Best Practices

Welcome to the part where we really dig into how to make Google Ads work for your home service business. We're discussing the nitty-gritty strategies and best practices that will turn your campaigns into lead-generating machines. Let's get started!

Pinpointing Your Audience: The First Step to Google Ads Success

A successful Google Ads campaign starts with understanding your target audience. You need to know exactly who you're trying to reach—whether it's homeowners needing emergency plumbing or businesses looking for regular HVAC maintenance. Use tools like Google Analytics to gather detailed insights about your audience and refine your targeting based on this data. The more specific you can be about who your ads are for, the more effective they will be.

Keyword Strategy: The Heart of PPC Campaigns

Google Ads are all about keywords. You can find the best keywords for your industry by using tools like Google's Keyword Planner. Start by identifying your potential customers' specific phrases when looking for home services. You want long-tail keywords with fewer competitors, so don't just target "plumbing services." Try "24-hour emergency plumbing services in Dallas."

Crafting Compelling Ad Copy and Choosing the Right Ad Format

Your ad copy needs to grab attention and compel viewers to take action. Highlight the benefits of your services, include a clear call-to-action, and make sure your ad is relevant to the search query. Experiment with different ad formats—search, display, and responsive—to see which perform best. Search ads are great for direct searches, while display ads can help with brand awareness by appearing on relevant websites.

Budgeting Smartly: Getting the Most Bang for Your Buck

Let's tackle the budget beast. You must allocate your budget wisely across different campaigns and ad groups. Don't be afraid to start small and scale up as you find what works. Use bid strategies like enhanced CPC (cost-per-click) or target CPA (cost-per-acquisition) to maximize ROI. Regularly review your spending and adjust your bids based on performance data.

Utilizing Ad Extensions

Ad extensions enhance your ads by providing additional information and increasing their visibility. To show your business address, use location extensions, which enable users to call you directly from the ad. Site link extensions provide links to specific pages on your website. These extensions can improve your ad's click-through rate and overall effectiveness.

Measuring Success: Tracking and Analytics

Use Google Analytics to better understand how your ads work. Track conversions to see which ads drive sales and leads. Track conversion, click-through, and cost-per-conversion metrics. Analyze this data regularly to improve your campaigns and refine your strategies.

Avoiding Common Pitfalls

Google Ads can be a money pit if not managed correctly. Avoid using Performance Max campaigns that can drain your budget quickly by appearing in irrelevant searches. Use negative keywords to filter out unwanted traffic. Continuously optimize your campaigns by testing different ad copy, keywords, and targeting options. You cannot just set Google Ads and forget about them; it requires constant monitoring and adjustment.

Following these strategies and best practices, you can create effective Google Ads campaigns that drive targeted traffic and generate quality leads for your home service business. Keep refining your approach, stay on top of your analytics, and don't be afraid to experiment with new tactics. With the right strategy, Google Ads can become a powerful tool in your marketing arsenal.

Local Service Ads: Leveraging Google's Power

Alright, buckle up! We're diving into the world of Google Local Services Ads (LSAs), also known as Google Guarantee. If you thought regular Google Ads were powerful, wait to see what LSAs can do for your home service business. These ads are designed to help local service providers, like appliance repair companies, get noticed and build trust with potential customers. Let's break it down.

Introduction to Google Local Services Ads

Google Local Services Ads are a game-changer for home service businesses. These ads appear at the very top of Google search results, even above the standard Google Ads. They're designed to connect local service providers with customers who need their services right now. The Google Guarantee badge makes LSAs particularly appealing, which builds instant trust and credibility with potential customers.

Setting Up Your Google Local Services Ads

Setting up LSAs may seem daunting, but it's pretty straightforward. Here's how to get started:

1. **Sign Up and Create Your Profile:** Head over to the Google Local Services Ads page and sign up. You'll need to provide basic information about your business, including your services, service areas, and contact details.

2. **Pass Background Checks:** Because Google values customer trust, any employee interacting with customers is required to pass background checks. This process helps ensure that customers are hiring reputable and reliable service providers.

3. **Get Your License and Insurance Verified:** You must provide proof of licensing and insurance to meet Google's requirements. This step is crucial for earning the Google Guarantee badge.

4. **Set Your Budget:** Determine your weekly ad budget. Unlike traditional advertisements, LSAs are pay-per-lead, which means you only pay when a customer contacts you.

5. **Customize Your Profile:** Add photos, business hours, and any other relevant information to make your profile stand out. A complete and detailed profile helps attract more customers.

Optimizing Your Local Services Ads for Maximum Impact

Once your LSAs are up and running, it's important to optimize them to ensure you're getting the best possible results. Here's how:

1. **Respond Quickly to Leads:** Google rewards businesses that respond quickly to customer inquiries. Make sure you're ready to answer calls and messages promptly to increase your chances of converting leads into customers.

2. **Collect and Showcase Reviews:** Positive reviews are crucial for building trust and attracting more

customers. Be sure to thank customers for their reviews and encourage them to leave them.

3. **Maintain a High Star Rating:** A high star rating can significantly impact your ad performance. Aim to provide excellent service consistently to keep your rating high.

4. **Update Your Profile Regularly:** Keep your profile information up-to-date, including your services, service areas, and business hours. This ensures customers have the most accurate information about your business.

Importance of Google LSA Reviews

Reviews are a cornerstone of your Google Local Services Ads (LSA) profile. Your ads are not only ranked and displayed by Google based on their quality but also their trustworthiness with potential customers. Leads and conversions can be increased when a profile has good reviews. Here's how reviews affect your LSA profile and the effectiveness of your ads.

Building Trust and Credibility

Positive reviews enhance your business's credibility and trustworthiness. Customers are more likely to choose your business over your competitors if they see that others have had good experiences with your services. A high star rating and detailed, positive feedback can significantly influence customer decisions.

Reviews Impact on Ad Ranking

Google uses reviews as a key factor in determining the ranking of Local Services Ads. The results of a search are more likely to feature profiles with high ratings and positive reviews. This visibility is crucial because it increases customers' likelihood of seeing and clicking on your ad.

Encouraging LSA Customer Reviews

To maximize the benefits of your LSA reviews, actively encourage your customers to leave feedback. After completing a job, kindly ask satisfied customers to share their experiences on your Google LSA profile. This is separate from your Google Business Profile reviews link. An email follow-up with the review page's link will make this process easier for your customers.

Disputing Charges for Bogus Leads: Updated Process

Sometimes, not all leads are legit. If you receive a bogus lead, don't fret—Google has a process for disputing these charges. Great news, home service business owners! Google simplified the process of getting credits for poor-quality leads from your Local Services Ads (LSAs). No more tedious manual disputes for every single questionable lead. With Google's new automatic crediting system, you'll be reimbursed faster and with much less effort.

Automatic Crediting

Google has introduced an automatic crediting system to replace the old manual lead dispute process. Here's how it works:

1. **Automatic Detection:** Google will now automatically identify and credit you for leads deemed poor in quality. This proactive approach means you don't have to manually dispute every lead that doesn't meet your criteria.

2. **Faster Credits:** Because the system is automated, you'll receive credits for bad leads much more quickly. This means you can focus more on your business and less on disputing charges.

3. **Feedback System:** While the automatic crediting system will handle most of the poor-quality leads, your feedback still matters. Google has introduced a new Lead Feedback Survey in your lead inbox. Use this survey to share your thoughts on individual leads. Although credits for "job type not serviced" and "geo not serviced" leads are discontinued, your feedback will help Google fine-tune the system to send you more of the leads you want and fewer of those you don't.

How to Use the Lead Feedback Survey

Even with automatic crediting, it's important to communicate with Google about the quality of the leads you're receiving. Here's how to use the new Lead Feedback Survey:

1. **Accessing the Survey:**

   - Log into your LSA dashboard.

   - Navigate to your lead inbox.

2. **Submitting Feedback:**

   - Select the lead you want to provide feedback on.

   - Fill out the survey with details about why the lead could have been better in quality. Be as clear and concise as possible.

3. **Impact of Your Feedback:**

   - Google will use your feedback to improve their lead matching algorithm.

   - Occasionally, you may still receive credits for leads reported as poor in quality through this survey.

Why These Changes Matter

Google found that many advertisers needed to take full advantage of the lead dispute process. By automating the crediting process, Google ensures that more businesses receive refunds for poor-quality leads without navigating a cumbersome dispute system. This improvement is designed to help you get the most out of your LSAs and focus on growing your business.

Local Services Ads from Google can be a powerful tool for reaching local customers and increasing your visibility. The new automatic crediting system has made managing your ad spend even easier. Remember to provide feedback on your leads to help Google continue to refine its system. By staying proactive and engaged with these tools, you'll be well on your way to maximizing the benefits of Google Local Services Ads.

CHAPTER 8

EMAIL MARKETING

Now, I know what you might be thinking: "Email? Isn't that a bit old-school?" Let me set things straight: email marketing is still relevant. In fact, it's one of the most powerful tools in your marketing arsenal, especially for home service companies. Imagine reaching out directly to past customers, re-engaging them with enticing offers, and encouraging repeat business, all with the click of a button. Sounds pretty great, right?

Get ready to revolutionize your marketing strategy. In this chapter, I'll guide you through the power of email marketing and how it can significantly increase your leads and sales. We'll cover everything from building and segmenting your email list, crafting effective email campaigns, and automating follow-ups. Plus, you'll learn the magic of email remarketing (or retargeting) and how targeting past customers can supercharge your marketing efforts.

So sit back and get ready to turn your inbox into a lead-generating machine. Let's get started!

Building and Segmenting Your List

Alright, folks, let's talk about the foundation of any successful email marketing campaign: your email list. The best way to reach your potential or past customers is by building an email list. It's your golden ticket to reaching out with personalized messages that can convert leads into loyal customers.

But it's not just about collecting emails; it's about segmenting your list so you can send the right message to the right person at the right time. Let's dive into how you can build and segment an email list that drives results for your home service business.

Building Your Email List

Start with Your Website

1. **Sign-Up Forms**: Display sign-up forms on the homepage, the blog, and the contact page of your website. Make it easy for visitors to subscribe to your newsletter or special offers. Remember, 47% of email recipients say they open an email based on the subject line alone, so keep your sign-up form enticing.

2. **Pop-Ups**: Use well-timed pop-ups to capture emails. Provide a discount or freebie in exchange for their email address. This can significantly boost your subscription rates.

Leverage Social Media

Promote your email sign-up on your social media platforms. Use engaging posts to encourage followers to join your email list for exclusive content and offers. A fun post with a call-to-action can drive followers to subscribe.

Run Contests and Giveaways

Host contests or giveaways that require participants to provide their email address to enter. This not only grows your list but also increases engagement with your brand. Everyone loves a good giveaway!

Utilize Offline Opportunities

Collect emails during service visits, at trade shows, or community events. A simple ask from a satisfied customer can go a long way. For example, after fixing a customer's HVAC system, ask if they'd like to sign up for maintenance reminders via Email.

Referral Programs

Make referrals even more effective by offering incentives like discounts or gift cards to their favorite restaurant for people who make a successful referral. Word-of-mouth can be powerful, and an incentive can work wonders.

Segmenting Your Email List

Once you have a growing list of subscribers, it's time to segment. Segmentation allows you to send more personalized and relevant emails, which can significantly increase your open and click-through rates. Your email list can be effectively segmented in the following ways:

Demographic Segmentation

- **Age, Gender, Location**: Basic demographic information can help tailor your messages. For instance, targeting by location ensures relevance if you're offering seasonal services. A whopping 98%

of millennials and Gen Xers rely on Email more than any other generation.

Behavioral Segmentation

- **Past Interactions**: Segment your list based on past interactions with your emails or website. For example, create a segment for subscribers who have clicked on a specific service but have yet to book.

Purchase History

- **Previous Customers**: Identify customers who have used your services before. Send them targeted offers for complementary services or maintenance reminders. With an overall ROI of 4,200% in email marketing, nurturing these relationships can be very profitable.

Engagement Level

- **Active vs. Inactive Subscribers**: Separate highly engaged subscribers from those who last opened your emails a while ago. Send re-engagement campaigns to inactive subscribers to win them back.

Customer Lifecycle Stage

- **New Leads, Current Customers, Lapsed Customers**: Tailor your messaging based on where the subscriber is in their journey with your business. New leads might need more educational content, while current customers might appreciate loyalty offers.

A good email marketing campaign depends on building and segmenting an email list. You can send targeted, relevant messages that resonate with your audience by collecting emails from many different channels and segmenting them thoughtfully. By using this approach, you can increase engagement rates and convert leads into loyal customers more effectively.

Get out there and start building and segmenting your list today!

Remember, details make the difference. With nearly 4.73 billion email users projected by 2026, the potential audience for your well-segmented and targeted campaigns is enormous. Keep refining your list, personalizing your messages, and watch your leads and sales grow.

Crafting Effective Email Campaigns

Alright, my friend, you've got your email list built and segmented, and now it's time to dive into the fun part: crafting those killer email campaigns. You want your emails to stand out in the crowded inbox, grab attention, and compel your readers to take action. But how do you do that?

Let's break it down with some email marketing best practices, tips for writing irresistible subject lines, compelling body content, powerful calls to action, and evading those pesky spam filters.

Email Marketing Best Practices

First things first, let's talk about some foundational email marketing best practices. These are your golden rules for ensuring your campaigns are effective and well-received.

1. **Personalization is Key:** Address subscribers by their names and personalize content according to their preferences. For example, "Hey John, we noticed your AC might need a check-up before summer hits."

2. **Keep It Concise:** People have short attention spans, especially when it comes to emails. Get to the point quickly and keep your emails concise and focused.

3. **Mobile-Friendly Design:** Most people check their emails on their phones, so make sure your emails look great on all devices. A responsive design is a must.

4. **Test and Optimize:** Regularly test different elements of your emails, from subject lines to call-to-action buttons, and use the data to optimize future campaigns.

Subject Lines

Your subject line is your first impression; as they say, you never get a second chance to make a first impression. Here are some tips to make your subject lines irresistible:

1. **Be Clear and Direct:** Let your readers know exactly what to expect. For example, "20% Off Your Next Plumbing Service – This Week Only!"

2. **Create Urgency:** Use time-sensitive language to create a sense of urgency. For instance, "Limited Time Offer: Book Your HVAC Service Today!"

3. **Add Personalization:** Including the recipient's name can make your email feel more personal. "Jane, Get Ready for Winter with Our Heating Services."

4. **Keep It Short:** Aim for 6-10 words. Short and sweet wins the race. "Special Offer Just for You, Mike!"

It's important to remember that 47% of email recipients open emails based on what the subject line says.

Writing Compelling Body Content

Now that you've grabbed their attention with your subject line let's keep them hooked with compelling body content:

1. **Start with a Strong Opening:** Kick off with a personalized greeting and a hook that draws them in. "Hi Sarah, is your fridge making strange noises? Here's how we can help."

2. **Provide Value:** Focus on how your service benefits the reader. "Our thorough HVAC maintenance ensures your home stays comfortable all year round, potentially saving you from costly repairs down the line."

3. **Tell a Story:** People love stories. Share a quick customer success story or a relatable scenario. "Last month, we helped a local family avoid a major flood by repairing their leaking pipe in time."

4. **Use Visuals:** Break up the text with images, infographics, or short videos. Visual content can increase engagement significantly.

Calls to Action

A powerful call to action (CTA) is crucial for converting readers into customers. Here's how to craft effective CTAs:

1. **Be Clear and Direct:** Tell your readers exactly what you want them to do. "Schedule Your Free Inspection Now."

2. **Create Fear Of Missing Out (FOMO):** Use phrases such as "Act Now," "Time is Limited," or "Don't Miss Out."

3. **Make It Stand Out:** Use buttons or bold text to make your CTA stand out visually. "Claim Your Discount Today!"

4. **Keep It Relevant:** Ensure your CTA aligns with the email content. If the email is about a special offer, the CTA should lead to that offer.

Evading the Spam Filters

You don't want your beautifully crafted email ending up in the spam folder. Here's how to avoid that fate:

1. **Avoid Spammy Language:** Words like "free," "urgent," and "guarantee" can trigger spam filters. Use them sparingly and contextually.

2. **Use a Recognizable Sender Name:** Make sure your sender name is recognizable and trustworthy. "ACME Appliance Repair" is better than "info@acmerepair.com."

3. Authenticate Your Domain: Use SPF, DKIM, and DMARC authentication to help ensure your emails are delivered to the inbox.

4. **Include an Unsubscribe Link:** Always include an easy way for recipients to unsubscribe. It's not just best practice; it's the law.

5. **Check Your Email's Spam Score:** Use tools to check the spam score of your emails before sending them out. Doing so lets you catch and fix any problems that could cause your email to be filtered as spam.

By following these tips and best practices, you can craft email campaigns that reach your audience and engage and convert them. So go ahead, put these strategies into action, and watch your home service business thrive through the power of email marketing!

Automation and Follow-Up

Let's be honest, juggling repairs, customer calls, and paperwork leaves little time for crafting the perfect email. That's where email marketing automation swoops in like a superhero, saving the day and your sanity! These tools streamline customer communication, nurturing leads and turning them into loyal fans. We will review the benefits of email marketing automation in this section and how it can be used to automatically send review requests after service calls.

The Benefits of Email Marketing Automation

First off, let's talk about why email marketing automation is your new best friend:

1. **Saves Time:** Automation tools handle repetitive tasks like sending follow-up emails and reminders, freeing up your time to focus on what you do best— providing excellent home services.

2. **Improves Customer Communication:** Automated emails ensure customers receive timely updates and information. Whether confirming an

appointment or thanking them for their business, automated communication keeps you top of mind.

3. **Increases Efficiency:** By automating your email marketing, you can ensure that no lead or customer falls through the cracks. Everyone gets the attention they need, which can significantly boost conversion rates and customer satisfaction.

4. **Enhances Personalization:** Many automation tools allow you to personalize your emails based on customer data, making your messages more relevant and engaging.

5. **Boosts Engagement:** Consistent, timely communication keeps your audience engaged and more likely to respond to your calls to action, whether booking a service or leaving a review.

Automation Tools Designed for Home Service Businesses

Here are some popular options designed with home service businesses in mind:

Housecall Pro

- **Features:** Automated email reminders and follow-ups for appointments, estimates, and invoices.

- **Benefits:** Reduces no-shows, improves customer communication, and streamlines payment collection.

- **Example:** Housecall Pro sends an automated reminder email two days before a scheduled appointment, reducing no-shows by up to 50%.

ServiceTitan

- **Features:** Email campaigns for lead nurturing, customer retention, and upselling.

- **Benefits:** Nurtures leads into paying customers, improves customer satisfaction, and drives repeat business.

- **Example:** ServiceTitan sends a personalized email to a customer who recently had their HVAC system serviced, offering a discount on a maintenance plan.

Jobber

- Features: Automated email follow-ups for quotes and invoices, customizable email templates, and email marketing campaigns.

- Benefits: Streamlines communication, saves time, and enhances professionalism.

- Example: Jobber sends a follow-up email to a customer who has yet to respond to a quote within a specified timeframe, increasing the chances of closing the deal.

Thryv

- **Features:** Automated email marketing, text message marketing, online reputation management, and social media management.

- **Benefits:** Provides a comprehensive solution for managing all customer communication and marketing aspects.

- **Example:** Thryv automatically solicits customers' reviews, helping businesses build their reputation.

Sending Automated Review Requests

After completing a service call, following up with your customers and requesting reviews is crucial. Here's how automation can help:

1. **Set Up Automated Triggers:** Configure your email automation tool to send a review request automatically once a service call is marked as completed in your system. This ensures every customer receives a prompt follow-up without you lifting a finger.

2. **Personalize Your Request:** Use the customer's name and reference the service performed. For example, "Hi John, we hope you're happy with the recent

HVAC maintenance service. We'd love to hear your feedback!"

3. **Include a Direct Link:** Provide a direct link to your Google, Yelp, or other platform review page so customers can easily leave reviews.

4. **Express Gratitude:** Thank your customers for their time and feedback. A simple "Thank you for your support!" can go a long way in making them feel appreciated.

Choosing the Right Tool

When choosing your best email marketing automation tool, you should consider your business needs and budget. Consider these factors:

- **Features:** What features are most important to you? Do you need automated reminders, customizable templates, or advanced email marketing campaigns?

- **Ease of Use:** How user-friendly is the platform? Can you easily create and send emails without technical expertise?

- **Integration:** Can the tool integrate your existing CRM or scheduling program? Your workflow will be streamlined, and time will be saved.

- **Price:** How much are you willing to spend? Email marketing automation tools come in a wide range of prices.

You can test out several of these tools for free before committing, which is the best part about them. Take advantage of these trials to find the perfect fit for your business.

Staying in touch with your customers, building stronger relationships, and ultimately growing your home service business can all be achieved through email marketing automation. So, embrace automation and watch your efficiency and customer satisfaction soar!

CHAPTER
9

A PEP TALK FROM YOUR COACH

Hey, champ! Look at you, making it halfway through this digital marketing marathon! I know, I know, reading about email automation and SEO can feel like you're going ten rounds with Apollo Creed.

It's a lot to take in, and your brain might feel like it's been hit with a left hook. But guess what? You're still standing, and that's what matters.

You're a home service hero, not a digital marketing guru, and that's perfectly okay. This stuff can be overwhelming and confusing, like trying to fix a leaky faucet in the dark. But you're doing great, and I'm here to tell you: keep pushing forward.

Think of this book as your training montage. Every email you send, every keyword you research, and every ad you optimize is another step closer to the top. You're not just learning about digital marketing; you're equipping yourself with the tools to knock out the competition and take your business to new heights.

Remember, Rocky didn't become the champ by giving up halfway through training. He persisted, even when it was challenging. And look at the results! So take a deep breath, clear the confusion, and get ready to jump back in. You have the strength to go the distance, and I'm right here in your corner, cheering you on.

Now, let's get back in the ring and finish this thing strong. You've got the heart of a champion, and with every new strategy you learn, you're getting closer to that title. Keep your eye on the prize, and let's make your home service business the heavyweight champ of digital marketing!

You got this, champ! Now, let's go show the digital world what you're made of.

CHAPTER

10

ANALYTICS AND MONITORING

Alright, my friend, you've made it this far, and now we're diving into numbers, charts, and data.

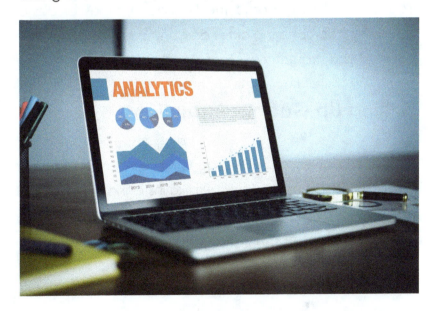

Consider this chapter your secret weapon for turning all those marketing efforts into tangible results. It's like having a radar for your business, showing you what's working, what's not, and where you need to pivot.

This chapter will cover three main points: setting up Google Analytics, tracking key metrics, and making data-driven decisions. Now, I know what you're thinking—"Great, more techy stuff to learn." But trust me, understanding analytics is like having the playbook for your favorite sports team. It's going to show you the winning moves and help you steer clear of any fumbles.

So, grab your coffee, put on your data goggles, and let's get ready to transform those numbers into knowledge that can power your home service business to new heights. You're about to become the Sherlock Holmes of digital marketing, deciphering clues and uncovering insights that will lead you straight to victory. Ready? Let's do this!

Setting Up Google Analytics

Alright, let's dive into setting up Google Analytics for your home service business. Think of it like installing a new HVAC system—you want to get it right the first time to ensure everything runs smoothly. Don't worry; I'll walk you through it step-by-step, and soon you'll be a data-tracking pro.

Step 1: Create a Google Analytics Account

First things first, you need a Google account. If you don't already have one, head over to Google and create one. Once you've got that sorted, go to the Google Analytics homepage and click on "Start for free."

1. **Sign Up for Google Analytics:** Click on "Start measuring" and enter your account name. This can be your business name.

2. **Set Up a Property:** Click on "Next" and set up a property. A property is basically your website. Enter the name of your website, its URL, and your time zone.

3. **Add Business Information:** Fill in your business details, such as industry category (like "Home Services") and the size of your business. This helps Google Analytics tailor the experience to your needs.

Step 2: Get Your Tracking ID

After setting up your property, you'll be given a tracking ID—a unique code you'll need to add to your website to start collecting visitor data.

1. **Find Your Tracking ID:** It should look something like "UA-12345678-1." Copy this ID.

2. **Install the Tracking Code:** This part might sound a bit techy, but it's crucial. You need to add this code to every page of your website. Here's how:

   - If you're using a website platform like WordPress, there are plugins (like "Insert Headers and Footers" or "MonsterInsights") that make this easy. Just paste the tracking ID into the plugin, and it'll handle the rest.

   - If you have a web developer, ask them to add the tracking code to the <head> section of your website's HTML.

Step 3: Verify Your Setup

To ensure everything is set up correctly, you must verify that Google Analytics is tracking your site properly.

1. **Go to Real-Time Reports:** In your Google Analytics dashboard, go to the "Real-Time" reports section. Open your website in a new browser tab.

2. **Check for Activity:** If everything is set up correctly, you should see real-time data indicating that someone (you) is on the site. If you see activity, congrats—you're good to go!

Step 4: Set Up Goals

Goals in Google Analytics help you measure how well your site fulfills your business objectives. For a home service company, this might be booking a service, filling out a contact form, or signing up for a newsletter.

1. **Navigate to Admin:** Click on the "Admin" gear icon in the bottom left corner.

2. **Set Up Goals:** Under the "View" column, click on "Goals" and then "New Goal."

3. **Choose a Template:** Select a goal template option that matches your goal type.

4. **Configure Your Goal:** Follow the prompts to set up your goal details. For instance, if your goal is booking a service, set the destination as the thank-you page URL users see after booking.

Step 5: Link Google Analytics with Google Ads

If you're running Google Ads (which you should be, considering all the great stuff we've covered about it), link your Google Ads account to Google Analytics to track ad performance.

1. **Go to Admin:** In the Admin section, click on "Google Ads Linking" under the "Property" column.

2. **Link Accounts:** Click on "+ New Link Group," select your Google Ads account, and follow the prompts to link the accounts.

And there you have it! Setting up Google Analytics might seem a bit intimidating at first, but once you've got it in place, it's like having a high-tech thermostat for your website—tracking performance and helping you make data-driven decisions to keep everything running smoothly. Now that you're set up, you can track key metrics and make informed choices to drive your home service business to new heights. Let's keep going and make the most out of this powerful tool!

Tracking Key Metrics

Now that you've set up Google Analytics, it's time to dive into the treasure trove of data at your fingertips. But with so much information available, it can be tough to know what to focus on. For a home service business, certain key performance indicators (KPIs) are especially important to track. Using these metrics, you can identify where you need to adjust your marketing efforts. Let's break down the essential KPIs you should be monitoring.

1. Website Traffic

Why It Matters: Website traffic is the lifeblood of your online presence. The more visitors you have, the more potential customers you can convert.

Metrics to Track:

- **Sessions:** The total number of visits to your site.

- **Users:** Visits to your site are counted as unique visitors.

- **Pageviews:** The total number of pages viewed on your site.

What to Look For: An upward trend in these metrics indicates growing interest and reach. Analyze which pages your audience is most interested in to determine what content resonates with them.

2. Source/Medium

Why It Matters: Understanding where your traffic comes from helps you identify which marketing channels are most effective.

Metrics to Track:

- **Organic Search:** Traffic from search engines.

- **Direct:** Traffic from people typing your URL directly into their browser.

- **Referral:** Traffic from links on other websites.

- **Social:** Traffic from social media platforms.

- **Paid Search:** Traffic from your Google Ads campaigns.

What to Look For: Identify which sources drive the most traffic and conversions. You can allocate your marketing budget more easily by using this method.

3. Bounce Rate

Why It Matters: When your bounce rate is high, it may indicate that your site isn't engaging or appealing to your customers. Bounce rate refers to the number of people visiting your site for one page before leaving.

What to Look For: Aim for a bounce rate below 50%. If it's higher, investigate which pages have the highest bounce rates and consider how to improve them. For instance, you can improve the bounce rate by making your website more user-friendly, adding engaging content, or optimizing your site's loading speed.

4. Conversion Rate

Why It Matters: The conversion rate measures the percentage of visitors who complete a desired action, such as booking a service or filling out a contact form. This is a direct indicator of your site's effectiveness at generating leads. To calculate the conversion rate, divide the number of goal completions by the number of sessions and then multiply by 100 to get the percentage.

Metrics to Track:

- **Goal Completions:** A measure of how many goals have been achieved (e.g., form submissions, bookings).

- **Goal Conversion Rate:** How many sessions led to goal completion.

What to Look For: Track conversion rates for different goals and pages to see where you're succeeding and where there might be bottlenecks.

5. Average Session Duration

Why It Matters: This metric shows how long visitors stay on your site. Longer sessions generally indicate higher engagement and interest in your content.

What to Look For: A higher average session duration suggests visitors find your content useful and engaging. If your average session duration could be higher, consider improving your content to keep visitors on your site longer.

6. Pages Per Session

Why It Matters: This metric measures the average number of pages viewed during a session. More pages per session often indicate a well-structured site with engaging content.

What to Look For: Strive for higher pages per session by providing clear navigation and compelling internal links that encourage visitors to explore more of your site.

7. Customer Lifetime Value (CLV)

Why It Matters: Understanding CLV helps you determine how much to spend on customer acquisition based on the amount of revenue your business can expect from a single customer account.

What to Look For: Track this metric over time to understand the long-term value of your customers and adjust your marketing strategies accordingly.

8. Return on Investment (ROI)

Why It Matters: ROI measures the profitability of your marketing efforts. It's essential for understanding your campaigns' effectiveness and making budget decisions.

Metrics to Track:

- Cost per Acquisition (CPA): The cost of acquiring a new customer.

- Revenue: The income generated from your services.

What to Look For: Compare your revenue to your marketing costs to determine your ROI. A positive ROI indicates that your campaigns are profitable.

By closely monitoring these key metrics, you'll gain valuable insights into your website's performance and overall marketing effectiveness. Making informed decisions, optimizing your strategies, and ultimately growing your home service business will be easier with this data-driven approach. So, roll up your sleeves, dive into those analytics reports, and start tracking your way to success!

Making Data-Driven Decisions

Alright, data nerds, it's time to talk about making data-driven decisions. You've got all these metrics from Google

Analytics, but here's a secret: not all metrics are created equal. It's easy to get lost in the sea of numbers, charts, and graphs, but the key is to focus on the data that truly matters for your business. Let's look at how to approach these insights wisely without becoming obsessed with every single statistic.

Understanding the Numbers

First and foremost, it's important to grasp the context behind the numbers. Metrics like page views, bounce, and conversion rates can provide valuable insights, but they must be understood in their specific context. Remember, Google Analytics is a tool, not a crystal ball. It offers estimates based on the data it collects, and while it's a powerful tool, it's not foolproof.

For example, let's say your bounce rate is high on a particular page. This might indicate that the content isn't engaging, but it could also mean visitors quickly found the information they needed and left. Instead of panicking and making drastic changes, dig deeper to understand the user behavior behind the numbers.

Focus on Actionable Insights

Not all metrics are created equal. Vanity metrics, such as sheer pageviews or the number of social media followers, may look impressive, but they don't always translate into business success. Instead, concentrate on actionable insights that directly align with your business objectives. This approach will help you prioritize your efforts and drive meaningful results.

For instance, if your goal is to increase service bookings, pay close attention to metrics like conversion rates, goal completions, and user flow. These metrics directly impact your bottom line and provide clear indicators of where improvements can be made.

Make Informed Adjustments

Data-driven decisions are about making informed adjustments rather than wholesale changes. Here's a step-by-step approach to using your data effectively:

1. **Identify a Metric to Improve:** Choose a specific metric that aligns with your business goals. For example, if you want to reduce bounce rates, focus on that metric.

2. **Hypothesize:** Develop a hypothesis about why the metric is underperforming. Maybe the page with a high bounce rate has slow loading times or irrelevant content.

3. **Make a Small Change:** Implement a small, manageable change based on your hypothesis. For instance, if you think the page is slow, optimize the images and scripts to improve loading times.

4. **Track the Results:** Monitor the impact of your change over time. Use Google Analytics to see if the bounce rate improves.

5. **Evaluate and Adjust:** If the change leads to improvement, consider implementing similar changes on other pages. If not, re-evaluate your hypothesis and try a different approach.

Avoiding Obsession with Metrics

It's easy to become obsessed with watching the numbers, but remember that data should serve as a guide, not a gospel. Here are a few tips to keep things in perspective:

- **Set Realistic Goals:** Establish clear, realistic goals for your metrics. Understand that improvement takes time and overnight success is rare.

- **Look for Trends, Not Blips:** Focus on long-term trends rather than daily fluctuations. A sudden spike or drop could be due to a variety of factors, so don't make hasty decisions based on short-term data.

- **Balance Data with Intuition:** While data is invaluable, don't ignore your business instincts and experience. You should use data to inform your business and customer decisions, but also trust your gut.

Examples of Smart Data-Driven Decisions

Example 1: Reducing Bounce Rates - You notice that your "Emergency Plumbing Services" page has a high bounce rate. After some investigation, you may find that the page loads slowly. You optimize the images and remove unnecessary scripts. Over the next month, the bounce rate decreases by 15%, and you see an uptick in service inquiries.

Example 2: Improving Conversion Rates - Your goal is to increase the number of bookings for your HVAC maintenance service. You add a clear call-to-action and a special discount offer on your landing page. By tracking the conversion rate, you see a 10% increase in bookings over the next quarter.

Making data-driven decisions is not just about using the right metrics to guide your actions, but about driving real business growth. You, as a data professional, have the power to make smart decisions that lead to tangible results. By understanding the numbers, focusing on actionable insights, making informed adjustments, and avoiding obsession with metrics, you can steer your business towards success. Keep experimenting, stay curious, and let your data lead you to success. Now, go out there and make those numbers work for you!

11

AUTOMATION AND AI IN MARKETING

AI isn't just a buzzword; it's revolutionizing how businesses operate, and if you're not on board, you're at risk of being left in the dust by competitors harnessing its power.

AI is reshaping the marketing landscape, from voice chatbots that qualify leads and schedule appointments to AI tools that generate content and optimize images and predictive analytics that can predict customer needs. This transformative power of AI is a game-changer for businesses.

For home service companies, embracing these technologies can mean the difference between staying competitive and getting left behind. AI tools can streamline your processes, enhance customer interactions, and provide previously unimaginable insights. So, buckle up as we explore how these cutting-edge technologies can help your business grow to a new level. It's time to embrace the future and ensure your business thrives in the AI-driven world. Let's get started!

Alright, let's talk about one of the coolest AI tools out there for home service businesses: AI voice chatbots for lead qualification and scheduling. Imagine having a virtual assistant who works 24/7, never takes a coffee break, and can handle multiple customer inquiries simultaneously. Sounds like a dream, right? Well, with voice chatbots, it's a reality.

AI Voice Chatbots for Lead Qualification and Scheduling

AI Voice Chatbots are transforming the way home service businesses interact with potential customers. They can qualify leads by asking pertinent questions, gathering customer information, and even scheduling appointments—all without any human intervention. This frees up your time and ensures no potential lead slips through the cracks.

For instance, services like **Air.ai** and **MyOfficeHelp.com** offer AI-powered voice chatbots designed to streamline customer service and scheduling processes. While I'm not endorsing these specific services, they are good examples of how voice chatbots can be utilized effectively in the home service industry.

How AI Voice Chatbots Work

An AI voice chatbot typically interacts with customers when you are unavailable to answer your phone. When a potential customer calls your business and starts a conversation, the chatbot can:

1. **Greet the Caller:** Provide a friendly welcome and ask how it can help.

2. **Qualify Leads:** Ask relevant questions to determine if the visitor is a viable lead. For example, it might ask

about the type of service needed, the preferred date and time, and contact information.

3. **Schedule Appointments:** Integrate with your scheduling system to book real-time appointments, ensuring your calendar is always up-to-date.

4. **Provide Information:** Answer common questions about your services, pricing, and availability.

Benefits of Using Voice Chatbots

1. **24/7 Availability:** Voice chatbots are always on, ensuring you take advantage of every opportunity to engage with a potential customer.

2. **Efficiency:** They can handle multiple inquiries simultaneously, which even the best human staff can struggle with.

3. **Consistency:** Provide consistent and accurate information every time, enhancing the customer experience.

4. **Cost-Effective:** Reduce the need for a large customer service team, saving on labor costs.

The Training Involved

However, it's important to note that implementing a voice chatbot isn't a plug-and-play solution. These bots require training to understand your business's specific needs and language. Here's what's involved:

1. **Initial Setup:** Configuring the chatbot to handle common inquiries and booking requests.

2. **Training the AI:** Teaching the chatbot to understand and reply appropriately to a wide range of customer questions. This can involve feeding it scripts, FAQs, and other relevant data.

3. **Ongoing Improvement:** Regularly updating the chatbot with new information and refining its responses based on customer interactions.

While voice chatbots are incredibly powerful, they are not perfect. At the writing of this book, this technology is still relatively in its infancy. AI technology is constantly improving rapidly, so I am sure it will improve more as time goes on. There may be instances where the bot doesn't understand a question or provides an incorrect response. Consider languages, accents, and regional dialects. Thick accents and dialects can really confuse a digital voice chatbot. Monitoring these interactions and adjusting as needed to improve the chatbot's performance is essential.

Incorporating voice chatbots for lead qualification and scheduling can significantly enhance your home service business's efficiency and customer satisfaction. While a fair amount of training is involved and may need improvement, the benefits far outweigh the initial effort. By adopting this technology, you'll be ahead of the curve, offering a seamless, always-on service that can help you capture more leads and keep your customers happy. So, why not give it a shot and see how chatbots can revolutionize your business operations?

AI Tools for Content Creation and Image Optimization

Alright, let's look into how AI is revolutionizing content creation and image optimization for home service businesses. Imagine having tools that can help you generate engaging blog posts, create stunning visuals, and optimize images for your website—all while saving you time and resources. Sounds amazing, right? Let's explore some of the top AI tools available and how they can benefit your business.

AI Content Creation Tools

Creating high-quality content is important for any business but can be time-consuming and challenging. AI tools for content creation can help streamline this process, making it easier to generate engaging and relevant content.

1. **Writesonic:** An AI writer that creates a wide range of content, including blog posts, ads, landing pages, product descriptions, and social media posts. It has a user-friendly interface and multiple templates.

2. **Copysmith:** This AI-powered platform focuses on creating high-converting marketing copy, including website copy, email campaigns, and social media ads. To optimize content performance, it offers features such as A/B testing and collaboration tools.

3. **Frase:** A comprehensive AI content platform that goes beyond content generation. It also helps with research, optimization, and analytics, making it a valuable tool for creating SEO-friendly content that ranks well in search engines.

4. **INK:** This AI writing assistant focuses on creating SEO-optimized content that is engaging and easy to read. It offers features like a readability checker, keyword optimization suggestions, and a built-in plagiarism checker.

5. **ChatGPT by OpenAI:** This tool can help you draft ideas for blog posts, social media updates, and

even customer emails. You provide a topic, and ChatGPT generates coherent, high-quality content. Make sure you are using the paid version of ChatGPT to get access to the most up-to-date release of the AI models.

6. **Copy.ai:** This platform uses AI to help you create marketing copy, blog ideas, and more. It's designed to assist with everything from headlines to full-length articles.

7. **Jasper (formerly Jarvis):** Jasper is another powerful AI writing tool that helps generate blog posts, marketing copy, and other written content quickly and efficiently.

8. **Google Gemini:** An AI tool by Google designed to generate high-quality content and integrate seamlessly with other Google services. It's useful for creating search-optimized content and leveraging Google's extensive data capabilities.

Example: Suppose you need a blog post about "Top Tips for Winterizing Your Home Plumbing." Using an AI tool like ChatGPT or Writesonic, you can generate a detailed, informative draft in minutes. After reviewing and editing the draft, you can add your own personal touch.

AI Image Optimization Tools

High-quality images are essential for engaging customers, but optimizing them can take time and effort. AI tools can help you enhance and optimize images for better website and social media performance.

1. **TinyPNG:** A popular tool that compresses PNG and JPEG images without significantly impacting their quality. Using it will help reduce image file sizes, resulting in faster website loading times.

2. **ShortPixel:** Similar to TinyPNG, this tool compresses images while preserving their visual quality. It offers bulk optimization options and integrates with popular content management systems like WordPress.

3. **Kraken.io:** This platform offers advanced image optimization features like lossy and lossless compression, resizing, and format conversion. It suits businesses requiring more control over their image optimization process.

4. **Canva:** While primarily a design tool, Canva uses AI to suggest design elements, layouts, and color schemes, making it easier to create visually appealing graphics.

5. **Adobe Spark:** Adobe's AI-powered tool helps create and optimize images for various platforms. It can suggest edits to enhance image quality and ensure it meets platform-specific requirements.

Example: Let's say you've taken photos of a recent HVAC installation. Using a tool like TinyPNG, you can compress these images to ensure they load quickly on your website. Meanwhile, Canva can help you create visually appealing before-and-after graphics to showcase your work on social media.

Embracing AI for Better Content and Images

With AI-powered content creation and image optimization tools, you will be able to create engaging and visually appealing content, saving time and resources while enhancing your marketing efforts. Despite the incredible power of these technologies, a human touch is still necessary to review and refine the AI-generated output to align perfectly with your brand voice and style.

In order to attract and retain customers, your home service business can create high-quality, engaging content using AI for content creation and image optimization. You can transform your marketing strategy with these AI tools, so why not give them a shot?

A Warning to the Wise

As fantastic as AI tools are, it's vital to remember that they aren't perfect. AI can generate content quickly, but it may need more nuance and understanding than a human touch provides. To ensure that your brand's content meets your standards, always review and edit artificially generated content. Unedited AI content can come across as generic, robotic, or even inaccurate, which can harm your brand's credibility.

With these AI tools, home service companies can create engaging content and visually appealing images that resonate with their target audiences, resulting in more website traffic, engagement, leads, and sales.

Predictive Analytics to Anticipate Customer Needs

Let's talk about predictive analytics and how it can transform your home service business. Consider what it would be like if you could anticipate a customer's needs before they even realized they needed your services. Sounds like magic, right? Well, with predictive analytics, it's pretty darn close.

What is Predictive Analytics?

Predictive analytics uses AI and machine learning algorithms to analyze historical data and make forecasts about future events. For home service companies, this means predicting when a customer might need a service, such as HVAC maintenance before a seasonal change or plumbing repairs, based on usage patterns. By leveraging these insights, you can proactively reach out to customers, schedule services, and stay ahead of potential issues.

How Home Service Companies Can Use Predictive Analytics

1. **Seasonal Maintenance:** Predictive analytics can help identify when customers will likely need seasonal services. For example, it can analyze past data to predict when HVAC systems typically need maintenance before summer and winter. This allows you to send timely reminders and offers to customers, ensuring their systems are in top shape when they need them most.

2. **Predicting Equipment Failures:** Predictive analytics can forecast potential equipment failures by analyzing usage patterns and service history. This is particularly useful for appliances like water heaters or air conditioning units. Knowing that a unit is likely to fail soon allows you to reach out with preventative maintenance offers, reducing the likelihood of emergency repairs and enhancing customer satisfaction.

3. **Optimizing Inventory Management:** Predictive analytics can also help in managing your inventory. By forecasting which parts and materials are likely needed based on upcoming service trends, you can ensure you have the right stock on hand. This reduces downtime and ensures faster service delivery to your customers.

4. **Customer Retention:** Predictive analytics allows you to identify patterns that indicate churning in clients. For example, if a customer hasn't booked a service in a while or has had a series of issues with their services, you can proactively reach out with special offers or personalized communication to re-engage them.

Implementing Predictive Analytics

To harness the power of predictive analytics, you'll need to invest in the right tools and technologies. Here are a few steps to get started:

1. **Collect Data:** The first step is gathering data. This includes service histories, customer interactions, seasonal trends, and any other relevant information. The more data you have, the more accurate your predictions will be.

2. **Choose the Right Tools:** A variety of AI-based tools are available to assist with predictive analytics. Some popular ones include IBM Watson, Google AI Platform, and Microsoft Azure Machine Learning. These tools can help analyze your data and provide actionable insights.

3. **Integrate with Your CRM:** You can leverage data more effectively if you integrate predictive analytics tools with your Customer Relationship Management (CRM) system. This integration ensures that insights

are readily available and can be acted upon quickly.

4. **Monitor and Adjust:** Predictive analytics isn't just set and forget. Continuously monitor the results and adjust your strategies based on the insights. This iterative process helps refine predictions and improve accuracy over time.

Real-World Examples

Example 1: HVAC Maintenance: A home service company analyzes data from past HVAC service calls using predictive analytics. The data shows that most customers need maintenance in early spring and late fall. The company sends out email reminders and offers discounted maintenance packages during these periods, resulting in increased bookings and customer satisfaction.

Example 2: Plumbing Services: A plumbing company predicts when water heaters are likely to fail by analyzing data on water heater lifespans and usage patterns. They proactively contact customers nearing this point with special offers for maintenance or replacement, reducing emergency calls and enhancing customer trust.

Predictive Analytics Solutions

Examples of AI-powered predictive analytics solutions that home service companies can leverage are:

Industry-Specific Platforms:

- **ServiceTitan:** Offers a comprehensive suite of tools for home service businesses, including AI-powered dispatching, scheduling, and customer management features that utilize predictive analytics.

- **Housecall Pro:** Provides a similar platform with predictive analytics capabilities for scheduling, marketing, and customer communication.

Customer Relationship Management (CRM) Systems with AI:

- **Salesforce Einstein:** Salesforce's AI component can be used to analyze customer data and predict behavior, enabling personalized recommendations and targeted marketing.

- **Zoho CRM:** Offers AI-powered features like Zia, a virtual assistant that can predict customer churn, identify cross-selling opportunities, and automate tasks.

Data Analytics and Business Intelligence Platforms:

- **Tableau:** Visualizes and analyzes data in-depth, making it easier to spot trends and patterns.

- **Microsoft Power BI:** An excellent data analytics tool for building predictive models and generating insights

Specialized Predictive Analytics Solutions:

- **Clari:** Focuses on revenue operations, using AI to forecast sales and identify opportunities for improvement.

- **RapidMiner:** A data science platform that enables businesses to build and deploy predictive models without knowing how to code.

You can stay ahead of customer needs by using predictive analytics, a powerful tool for home service companies. Using historical data and artificial intelligence algorithms, you can forecast future service needs, optimize inventory, and retain customers. By anticipating and meeting customer needs proactively, you can increase business efficiency and satisfaction, even though it requires data collection and technology investments.

So, embrace the power of predictive analytics and watch your home service business thrive in the AI-driven future!

CHAPTER

12

SCALING YOUR
MARKETING EFFORTS

Here's where we take your marketing game from local hero to regional rockstar. If you've ever dreamed of seeing your home service company's trucks in every neighborhood and your name on everyone's lips, buckle up, because this chapter is for you. We're talking about scaling your marketing efforts and taking things to the next level.

In this chapter, we'll explore three primary topics: Identifying New Opportunities, Expanding Your Service Area, and Partnering with Other Home Service Providers. Think of it as your playbook for growth, filled with strategies that can help you broaden your reach and maximize your impact. And don't worry—we'll keep it casual and sprinkle in some humor to make the ride enjoyable.

Whether you're an appliance repair, plumber, electrician, or HVAC expert, scaling your business doesn't have to feel like rocket science. It's all about finding the right opportunities, expanding strategically, and building strong partnerships. Ready to turn your local success into regional dominance? Let's get started!

Identifying New Opportunities

Imagine Busy Bob's Plumbing, a thriving home service company with three trucks zipping around town, fixing leaks and unclogging drains. Bob, the owner, has built a solid reputation, but lately, he's been feeling a bit stifled. Each day feels like a relentless race to keep up with calls, manage his team, and keep the paperwork flowing. In the chaos, it's easy to miss the untapped growth opportunities right under his nose.

One morning, over his steaming cup of coffee, Bob envisions a fourth truck serving a neighboring town. But is this a wise expansion? How can Bob determine if this new area is a goldmine or a money pit?

Step 1: Unearthing Market Demand

Bob's first mission is to uncover whether there's sufficient demand in the new area. He turns to the internet, his trusty detective tool:

- **Google Trends:** Bob can gauge relative interest levels by comparing search trends for "plumber" or "emergency plumbing" in his current and potential service areas. Are folks in the neighboring town actively seeking plumbing services?

- **Local Forums & Social Media:** Scouring online communities reveals common pain points. Are residents complaining about frequent leaks or lackluster service? Such insights offer valuable clues about unmet needs.

- **Census Data & Demographics:** Examining demographic data (age of homes, income levels) helps Bob understand if the area aligns with his ideal customer profile.

Step 2: Sizing Up the Competition

Next, Bob needs to scope out his potential rivals:

- **Competitor Websites & Online Presence:** Bob thoroughly examines competitors' websites and social media pages. Are they responsive? Do their reviews paint a positive picture? This intel reveals their strengths and weaknesses, highlighting areas where Bob can differentiate himself.

- **Local Directories:** Checking platforms like Yelp and Angie's shows how many plumbers are already operating in the area and how they are rated. Are there gaps in service offerings or underserved neighborhoods that Bob can tap into?

Step 3: Assessing Digital Marketing Potential

To truly conquer this new market, Bob evaluates the digital landscape:

- **Keyword Research:** Armed with tools like SEMrush or Ahrefs, Bob identifies relevant search terms. A high search volume with low competition suggests untapped potential. Are people searching for "24/7 plumber near me" but not finding many options?

- **Paid Advertising:** A small-scale Google Ads campaign targeted to the new area acts as a litmus test. If clicks and leads flow in, it signifies a receptive audience.

- **Local SEO:** Is there an opportunity to claim a top spot in local search results by optimizing his website and Google My Business listing for the new area?

Step 4: Validating with Real-World Tests

Before fully committing, Bob dips his toes in the water:

- **Introductory Offers:** A limited-time discount for new customers in the neighboring area, promoted through social media and local channels, can generate buzz and gauge interest.

- **Partnerships:** Teaming up with local businesses (real estate agents, property managers) can open doors to new customers and referral networks. We'll talk more about this later in this chapter.

Bob can systematically identify and validate new opportunities by meticulously following these steps without risking it all. Remember, even the busiest business owners need to step back and assess the landscape. For Bob, that fourth truck might be the key to unlocking a whole new chapter of growth. The possibilities are out there for you too, just waiting to be discovered.

Expanding Your Service Area

So, you've identified new opportunities, and you're ready to take your home service business to the next level by expanding your service area. This is an exciting move, but it comes with its own set of challenges and considerations. Let's walk through what it really takes to expand your service area effectively and in line with best practices.

Understanding the Limits of Google Business Profiles

First off, let's talk about Google Business Profiles (GBPs). These profiles are fantastic for boosting your local search visibility, but they have their limitations. Google has tightened up the proximity reach of GBPs, meaning your profile will primarily appear in searches close to your listed business address. If you want to expand into a new area, you might need more than just your existing GBP to cut it.

While digital marketing can certainly expand your reach, it's important to remember that GBP listings are optimized for local searches. This means your reach is typically limited to a certain radius around your physical location. A more strategic approach is often necessary to truly expand your service area and tap into new markets.

Establishing a Physical Presence

One of the best strategies for expanding your service area is establishing a small office in the center of the new service area. This provides a legitimate physical address that you can use to create a new Google Business Profile, thereby extending your local reach.

1. **Choosing the Location:** Find a location central to the new service area you want to target. This doesn't have to be a large office—just a space that can serve as a base for your operations and meet

Google's requirements for a physical business location.

2. **Setting Up the Office:** Ensure that this office has signage, a dedicated phone line, and business hours that match your service offerings. Google checks for these elements to verify the legitimacy of your business location.

Don't look at the cost of a new office as a determining factor. This is an investment in your business. If all of the other numbers add up from your market research, then your ROI for the office space should be more than worth it. Remember this is a long game, not a quick overnight return. So you need to be willing to invest for a bit before seeing a return on that investment.

Google's Guidelines and Best Practices

You should adhere to Google's guidelines when establishing your new home service location to avoid penalties or negative impacts on your online visibility. Here are some key points to remember:

1. **Accurate Address:** Ensure the address you provide for your new location accurately reflects the actual physical location of your office or satellite space. PO boxes or virtual addresses are not allowed.

2. **Staffed Location:** The new location should be staffed during your stated business hours. This means having employees or representatives available to answer

calls, schedule appointments, and meet with customers. Now this is just what Google wants, but let's face it, nobody does it.

3. **Clear Signage:** Display clear signage with your business name and logo at the new location. This reinforces your presence in the area and makes it easier for customers to find you.

4. **Local Phone Number:** Use a local phone number for the new location. This further solidifies your connection to the area and makes it more convenient for local customers to contact you.

5. **Separate GBP Listing:** Create a separate GBP listing for the new location, ensuring the information is accurate and consistent with your other listings. Avoid duplicating content across listings. And remember to create the new listing under a SEPARATE Google Account.

By following these guidelines, you can expand your service area effectively and ethically, building a strong online presence in your new market while adhering to Google's best practices.

Expanding your service area by setting up a new office and creating a Google Business Profile for that location can significantly boost your business's reach and growth. By carefully planning your expansion, adhering to Google's guidelines, and following best practices, you can successfully tap into new markets, grow your customer base, and increase your overall revenue. So, go ahead and take that next big step—you've got this!

Partnering with Other Home Service Providers

Alright, you're considering partnering with other home service providers, but how does this fit into your digital marketing strategy? Great question! Partnering with other home service providers can significantly amplify your digital marketing efforts by expanding your reach, increasing your credibility, and creating more content opportunities. Let's look at how these partnerships can be a game-changer for your business.

The Power of Strategic Partnerships

Imagine Busy Bob's Plumbing teaming up with a local HVAC company, an electrical service, and a landscaping business. These aren't just random connections but strategic partnerships that can drive mutual growth. Here's how:

1. **Referral Networks:** By partnering with other reputable home service providers, you create a referral network. When an HVAC technician notices a plumbing issue, they can refer the client to Busy Bob's Plumbing and vice versa. This boosts your client base and builds trust within the community.

2. **Joint Marketing Campaigns:** Pooling resources for joint marketing campaigns can be highly effective. You can co-sponsor local events, create bundled service packages, or run collaborative social media campaigns. This not only splits the cost but also broadens your audience.

3. **Content Collaboration:** Collaborating on content is a fantastic way to enhance your digital marketing. You can write blog posts, create videos, or host webinars together. For example, a blog post on "Preparing Your Home for Winter" could feature tips from a plumber, an HVAC technician, and an electrician. This adds value for your readers and boosts SEO.

Implementing Digital Marketing Strategies Through Partnerships

1. **Co-Branded Content:** Create co-branded content that showcases the expertise of all partners. This could include how-to guides, maintenance checklists, or seasonal tips. Sharing this content on your individual websites and social media channels increases visibility and engagement.

2. **Social Media Takeovers:** Host social media takeovers where partners take turns featuring each other's services on their profiles. For instance, Busy Bob's Plumbing could take over the HVAC

company's Instagram daily, sharing plumbing tips and promoting services. Your brand gets exposure to new people through this cross-promotion.

3. **SEO Benefits:** Backlinks are crucial for SEO. You create valuable backlinks by writing guest posts for each other's blogs or featuring each other on your websites. Your websites will rank higher and increase shared organic traffic.

4. **Email Marketing Collaborations:** Partner up for email marketing campaigns. For example, you could send out a joint newsletter featuring special offers from all partner companies. This not only provides value to your subscribers but also introduces them to complementary services.

Examples of Successful Partnerships

Example 1: The Winter Prep Package

Busy Bob's Plumbing partners with an HVAC company and an electrical service to offer a comprehensive "Winter Prep Package." Customers who book this package receive discounted rates on plumbing inspections, furnace tune-ups, and electrical system checks. This package is promoted through a joint social media campaign, email blasts, and co-branded blog posts, driving increased traffic and bookings for all companies involved.

Example 2: Home Maintenance Webinar

Bob and his partners decide to host a free webinar on home maintenance tips. Each partner covers their area of expertise, providing valuable advice to homeowners. The webinar is promoted across all their digital channels, and attendees are encouraged to follow each business on social media and subscribe to their newsletters for more tips. This collaborative effort boosts engagement and positions all the partners as experts in their fields.

Partnering with other home service providers is not just about sharing customers; it's about amplifying your digital marketing efforts. As a result of these partnerships, more effective email marketing campaigns can be created, backlinks can increase SEO, and social media can reach a broader audience. Together, you can increase visibility, attract more clients, and grow your businesses. So, start building those strategic alliances and watch your digital marketing efforts soar!

ADVANCED SEO TECHNIQUES

Welcome to the SEO geek-fest, folks! If you thought the previous chapters were a wild ride, buckle up because we're about to go deep into the technical trenches of SEO. I absolutely love SEO—there, I said it! There's something thrilling about getting into the nitty-gritty, geeky technical stuff that makes search engines tick. This will be the longest chapter in the book because there's just so much to cover, and I want to do it justice. So settle in, and let's embark on this epic journey together.

First up, we'll tackle the all-important technical website audit. This is your foundation, the bedrock of a solid SEO strategy. We'll look at how to dissect your site's structure, identify issues, and optimize for better performance. Next, we'll dive into SEO competitor analysis. Do you ever wonder why your competitors rank higher than you? I'll show you how to spy on your competition and leverage their strategies to boost your own rankings.

Then, we'll plunge into a keyword research deep dive. Finding the right keywords isn't enough; understanding how search terms fit into user intent is key. Speaking of user intent, we'll explore how to align your content with what your audience is really looking for, ensuring you meet their needs at every turn.

To make sure you're armed with the best tools, we'll cover various keyword research tools that can make your life a whole lot easier. And because we're all about that technical finesse, we'll get into schema markup—those little snippets of code that can make a big difference in how search engines understand your site.

It's impossible to write an SEO guide without mentioning backlinks. Here, we'll look at how to earn high-quality links to get your site to the top. And we'll finish up with tips on staying on top of algorithm changes. For long-term success, SEO needs to stay ahead of the curve.

Ready to geek out with me? Let's dive into the wonderful world of advanced SEO techniques. Remember, this is not just a one-way lecture. I encourage you to apply these strategies to your digital marketing game and see the results yourself. Together, we can take your digital marketing game to the next level!

Technical Website Audit

Let's roll up our sleeves and conduct a technical SEO audit, meticulously examining your website's inner workings. It is a comprehensive check-up to diagnose and resolve any underlying issues hindering your site's performance. This audit focuses solely on the website itself, pinpointing errors and areas for improvement that directly impact your on-page SEO.

1. Crawlability and Indexability: Opening the Doors to Search Engines

Ensure search engines can effortlessly crawl and index your site. If they can't access your pages, they won't rank them. Here's what to check:

- **XML Sitemap:** Make sure your XML sitemap is up-to-date and comprehensive, and submit it to search engines such as Bing Webmaster Tools and Google Search Console.

- **Robots.txt File:** Verify that it's not unintentionally blocking crucial pages or resources from search engine bots.

- **Crawl Errors:** Regularly monitor Google Search Console and Bing Webmaster Tools for 404 errors (page not found), 5xx server errors, and redirect loops.

- **URL Parameters:** Check if unnecessary URL parameters are causing duplicate content issues and address them with canonical tags or parameter handling in your CMS.

2. Site Speed and Performance: The Need for Speed

Page load speed is paramount for both user experience and search engine rankings.

- **Core Web Vitals:** These metrics (Largest Contentful Paint, First Input Delay, Cumulative Layout Shift) measure your site's loading performance, interactivity, and visual stability. Aim for "Good" scores across the board.

- **Image Optimization:** Compress images without sacrificing quality using tools like TinyPNG, ShortPixel, or ImageOptim. Consider newer formats like WebP for further optimization.

- **Caching:** Leverage browser caching and server-side caching to store static elements and reduce load times for repeat visitors.

- **Content Delivery Network (CDN):** Distribute your site's content across multiple servers globally to speed up delivery for users in different locations.

- **Minification:** Reduce the size of CSS, JavaScript, and HTML files by removing unnecessary characters and whitespace.

3. Mobile-Friendliness: Catering to the On-the-Go Audience

Most users search the Internet from their mobile devices, so it's important to have a mobile-friendly site. Google uses mobile crawlers to index pages, and if your website is not mobile friendly or has technical errors, Google will decide it is not indexable.

- **Mobile Usability Report:** Google Search Console provides valuable insights into mobile-specific issues like viewport configuration errors, small font sizes, or elements that are too close together.

- **Responsive Design:** Ensure your site adapts seamlessly to various screen sizes and resolutions.

- **Touchscreen Usability:** Buttons and links should be appropriately sized and spaced for easy tapping.

4. HTTPS and Security: Building Trust and Protecting Data

- **SSL Certificate:** An SSL certificate encrypts data transmitted between your site and users, boosting security and potentially improving rankings.

- **Mixed Content Warnings:** Resolve any instances where insecure (HTTP) elements are loaded on secure (HTTPS) pages.

- **Security Headers:** Implement headers like HSTS (HTTP Strict Transport Security) and CSP (Content Security Policy) to enhance security and protect against attacks.

5. URL Structure: Creating Clear Paths for Users and Bots

- **Descriptive URLs:** Use clear, concise URLs that include relevant keywords and accurately reflect the page's content.

- **Keyword-Rich URLs:** Optimize the URL with your target keywords after the domain name (the slug).

- **Lowercase Letters:** Stick to lowercase letters for consistency and avoid potential duplicate content issues.

- **Separators:** Use hyphens (-) to separate words in URLs, as underscores (_) may not be recognized as separators by some search engines.

6. On-Page SEO Elements: Guiding Search Engines

- **Title Tags:** Unique, descriptive, and compelling titles that include primary keywords.

- **Meta Descriptions:** Concise summaries of page content, enticing users to click through from search results.

- **Header Tags (H1-H6):** Properly structured headings clearly define content hierarchy and incorporate relevant keywords.

7. Internal Linking: Creating a Web of Connections

- **Strategic Internal Linking:** Make use of internal links to highlight important pages on your site, to distribute link equity, and to guide users through your site.

- **Anchor Text:** Use descriptive anchor text that accurately reflects the linked page's content.

- **Contextual Relevance:** Ensure internal links are placed within relevant context to enhance user experience.

8. Duplicate Content: Addressing Identity Crises

- **Canonical Tags:** To consolidate duplicate content signals, specify which version of a page is preferred.

- **301 Redirects:** Permanently redirect duplicate or outdated pages to the appropriate canonical versions.

- **Content Consolidation:** Merge or remove duplicate pages that serve no unique purpose.

- **Parameter Handling:** Manage URL parameters to prevent duplicate content issues caused by tracking codes or filters.

9. Structured Data and Schema Markup: Enhancing Visibility

- **Schema Markup:** Implement schema markup to provide search engines additional context about your content, potentially leading to rich snippets in search results.

- **Local Business Schema:** If applicable, mark up your business information with local business schema to enhance local SEO efforts.

- **FAQPage Schema:** If you have an FAQ page, use FAQPage schema to make your answers eligible for rich results.

- **Service Schema:** Service schema should be used on every service page of your website. This tells search engines that this is about a service rather than a typical blog post or city page.

10. Additional Technical Considerations:

- **Site Architecture:** Make sure your site is organized logically, so both users and search engines can find what you're looking for.

- **Broken Links:** Make sure that internal and external links are working properly, and fix them as necessary.

- **Hreflang Tags:** If your site targets multiple languages, implement hreflang tags to signal the correct language version to search engines.

- **XML Sitemap Validation:** Validate your XML sitemap using tools like the W3C XML Sitemap Validator to ensure it is error-free.

Tools for Conducting a Technical SEO Audit:

- **Google Search Console:** Your go-to resource for identifying crawl errors, indexing issues, and performance data.

- **Bing Webmaster Tools:** A similar platform to Google Search Console, offering valuable insights into your site's performance in Bing search.

- **Screaming Frog SEO Spider:** A powerful website crawler that helps identify a wide range of technical SEO issues.

- **SEMrush**: Provides in-depth website audits and actionable insights.

- **Website Auditor**: Offers detailed technical SEO audits and optimization tips.

- **Ahrefs:** Evaluates your website and provides a website health score.

- **DeepCrawl:** Another excellent website crawler with advanced features like log file analysis and JavaScript rendering.

- **GTmetrix:** Analyze your site's speed and performance with detailed recommendations for improvement.

- **Lighthouse:** An open-source tool integrated into Google Chrome that audits your site's performance, accessibility, and SEO.

- **Sitebulb:** A visual website crawler that provides a comprehensive overview of your site's structure and technical health.

SEO audits are essential for optimizing your site. With the right tools, you can improve crawlability, indexability, speed, mobile-friendliness, and overall user experience on your site, which leads to better search rankings and more organic traffic. If your website is healthy, it's going to get more visitors and customers.

SEO Competitor Analysis

It's time to unleash your inner detective and delve into the fascinating world of SEO competitor analysis. Understanding your competitors' online strategies gives you invaluable insights to refine your SEO game plan and climb higher search rankings. Let's explore the methods and tools that empower you to perform a thorough SEO competitor analysis.

Why Perform an SEO Competitor Analysis?

Before we dive into the "how," let's briefly address the "why." Analyzing your competitors can unlock numerous benefits:

- **Uncover Hidden Opportunities:** Spot gaps in your own SEO strategy, revealing areas where you can outshine your rivals.

- **Expand Your Keyword Arsenal:** Discover new keywords your competitors are ranking for, expanding your reach to a wider audience.

- **Benchmark Your Performance:** Understand your strengths and weaknesses relative to your competitors, enabling you to focus on areas for improvement.

- **Learn from Their Success (and Mistakes):** Analyze their content, backlink profiles, and technical SEO to replicate their winning tactics and avoid their mistakes.

Methods for SEO Competitor Analysis:

- **Identify Your True Competitors:** Your true SEO competitors aren't always the same businesses you compete with in the physical world. They are the websites vying for the same keywords and search visibility. To find them:

- **Google Search:** Conduct searches for your primary services in your target locations. The websites appearing in the top results are your direct competitors.

- **SEO Tools:** Use tools like Semrush, Ahrefs, or SpyFu to uncover direct and indirect competitors based on shared keywords and audience overlap.

- **Industry Resources:** Explore online directories, industry associations, and review sites to identify additional competitors.

Reverse Engineer Their Keyword Strategies

Keywords are the building blocks of SEO. Analyzing your competitors' keyword choices is crucial.

- **Keyword Research Tools:** Leverage tools like Semrush, Ahrefs, or Moz to reveal the keywords your competitors target and rank for.

- **Keyword Gap Analysis:** Identify keywords your competitors rank for that you still need to explore. These represent untapped opportunities to attract new visitors.

- **Search Intent:** Analyze the types of content your competitors create for different keywords. Are they informational blog posts, product pages, or local service landing pages? This helps you understand the user's intent behind each search and tailor your content accordingly.

Deconstruct Their Content Strategy

Content reigns supreme in SEO. Studying your competitors' content offers a wealth of inspiration.

- **Content Audit:** Evaluate your competitors' website content, blog posts, and social media presence. What topics do they cover extensively? Which content formats (articles, videos, infographics) do they use?

- **Content Gap Analysis:** Look for topics they still need to address or areas where you can create superior content. This could be a comprehensive guide, a unique case study, or an engaging video tutorial.

- **Quality and Engagement:** Assess their content's readability, depth, and overall quality. Look at social shares, comments, and backlinks to gauge audience engagement.

1. **Examine Their Backlink Profile:**

Search engines love links from other sites because they're like votes of confidence.

- **Backlink Analysis Tools:** Semrush, Ahrefs, and Moz offer comprehensive backlink analysis features. Analyze how authoritative and relevant the websites that link to your competitors are.

- **Competitor Backlink Gap:** Uncover websites linking to your competitors but not to you. These are potential targets for outreach and link-building.

- **Link Building Strategies:** Analyze the types of links your competitors are earning (e.g., guest posts, directory listings, resource page mentions). Replicate their successful strategies to build a strong backlink profile for your own site.

Assess Their Technical SEO

Technical SEO lays the groundwork for a high-performing website. Evaluate your competitors' technical aspects to find areas where you can outpace them.

- **Site Speed:** Use tools like GTmetrix or PageSpeed Insights to compare your site's loading speed with your competitors. A faster site often leads to better rankings and user experience.

- **Mobile-Friendliness:** Prioritize mobile-friendly design for your website, as most users now browse and search from their phones. Your mobile performance can be assessed by Google's Mobile-Friendly Test.

- **Core Web Vitals:** These metrics (Largest Contentful Paint, First Input Delay, Cumulative Layout Shift) are crucial for both user experience and search rankings. Analyze your competitors' Core Web Vitals scores and aim to match or exceed them.

- **Site Architecture:** Study your competitors' site structure, internal linking, and use of structured data to optimize your own site's architecture for better crawlability and indexability.

When you consistently conduct SEO competitor analysis and use these tools, you can gain an edge in the home service industry. You can optimize your SEO strategy, create exceptional content, and ultimately attract more qualified customers and leads by understanding your rivals. In the digital world, knowledge is power, and competitor analysis will help you unlock it.

Keyword Research Deep Dive

In SEO, keywords bridge what your potential customers are searching for and the solutions your home service business offers. Thorough keyword research goes beyond simply identifying popular search terms; it involves understanding the nuances of language, user intent, and the relationships between words. Let's take a deep dive into keyword research, exploring semantic relationships, entities, user intent, and the array of tools available to aid your quest.

Semantically Related Terms and Entities: Beyond Exact Match Keywords

Modern search engines like Google have evolved to understand the meaning behind words rather than relying solely on exact matches. This means you need to expand your keyword research beyond just single terms and consider semantically related terms and entities.

- **Semantically Related Terms**: These are words or phrases that are closely related in meaning to your target keywords. For example, "leaky faucet" and "dripping tap" are semantically related for a plumber. Including these variations in your content helps search engines understand the broader context of your services.

- **Entities**: Entities are specific things, people, or places that search engines recognize as distinct concepts. For instance, "Chicago" is an entity, as are "plumber" and "drain cleaning." Incorporating entities into your content can enhance its relevance and visibility for search queries related to those entities.

User Intent: Matching Content to Needs

Understanding user intent is crucial for successful keyword research. What are your potential customers actually looking for when they type in a particular search query?

Are they seeking information, looking to make a purchase, or trying to find a local business?

- **Informational Intent**: Users seeking information typically use keywords like "how to fix a leaky faucet" or "signs of a clogged drain." Your content should aim to educate and provide helpful solutions to these problems.

- **Transactional Intent**: Users ready to buy may use keywords like "emergency plumber near me" or "book a drain cleaning service." Your content should highlight your services, showcase your expertise, and make it easy for them to contact you.

- **Local Intent**: Users looking for local businesses often include their location in search queries, like "plumber in Chicago." Optimize your website and Google Business Profile for local SEO to capture these searches.

Keyword Placement: Where to Use Keywords on Your Page

Keywords should be strategically placed in various locations on your page to maximize their impact. There are 13 key areas where keywords can be effectively used:

1. **Meta Title/Page Title**: Ensure your target keyword is included in the title tag, ideally near the beginning, for maximum impact.

2. **H1 Tag**: Your main heading should feature your primary keyword, providing a clear signal to search engines about the page's content.

3. **Body Content**: Naturally incorporate your keywords throughout the body content, maintaining a good keyword density without overstuffing.

4. **URL**: Include the keyword in the page URL to enhance relevance and improve click-through rates.

5. **H2, H3, H4 Tags**: Use secondary headings to structure your content, including variations or related keywords.

6. **Anchor Text**: Use keyword-rich anchor text in internal links to strengthen the internal link structure.

7. **Bold and Italic Text**: Emphasize keywords in bold or italics to highlight important points, aiding readability and SEO.

8. **Image Alt Text and File Names**: Optimize images by including keywords in the alt text and file names.

9. **Schema Markup**: Implement schema markup that includes keywords to enhance search engine understanding and result display.

10. **Open Graph Tags**: Use keywords in Open Graph tags to improve how your content appears when shared on social media.

11. **HTML Tags**: Ensure keywords are present in various HTML elements where relevant.

12. **Above the Fold**: Place keywords early in the content (above the fold) to catch attention and emphasize importance. Incorporate keywords within the first 100 words of your content for better prominence and relevance.

13. **Main Menu**: You can also include your primary keywords within your menus.

Using Keyword Modifiers

Keyword modifiers are additional words that enhance the main keyword to target specific search intents or contexts. Using keyword modifiers can help you capture more targeted traffic and improve the relevance of your content.

- **Location-Based Modifiers**: Adding locations to your keywords, such as "Chicago plumber" or "emergency plumbing in New York," helps target local searches.

- **Service-Based Modifiers**: Specify the type of service, like "commercial plumbing repair" or "residential drain cleaning."

- **Intent Modifiers**: Words like "best," "top," "cheap," "affordable," and "emergency" cater to different user intents and can attract more qualified leads.

For example, instead of just targeting "plumber," you could use modifiers to target "best emergency plumber in Chicago" or "affordable drain cleaning service."

Keyword Prominence and Density

- **Keyword Prominence**: Keywords should appear early in your content and be placed close together to signal strong relevance to search engines.

- **Keyword Density vs. Word Count**: Maintaining a balanced keyword density is more important than simply increasing word count. Ensure keywords are used naturally without overstuffing.

Keyword Research Tools: Your Arsenal for Discovery

A wide range of keyword research tools are available, both free and paid, to aid your quest for the perfect keywords:

Free Keyword Research Tools

- **Google Keyword Planner**: A fundamental tool for understanding search volume and keyword competition. It's primarily designed for advertisers but can also be useful for SEO.

- **AnswerThePublic**: Uncovers questions people are asking about your topic, providing valuable insights into user intent and long-tail keyword opportunities.

- **Keyword Surfer**: A free Chrome extension that displays estimated search volume and related keywords directly in Google search results.

- **Google Search Console**: Provides data on the keywords your website is already ranking for, helping you identify opportunities for optimization and content expansion.

Paid Keyword Research Tools

- **Semrush**: A comprehensive SEO platform offering in-depth keyword research, competitor analysis, and rank-tracking features.

- **Ahrefs**: Another powerful SEO toolset with extensive keyword research capabilities, including a vast database of keyword ideas and backlink analysis.

- **Moz Keyword Explorer**: A user-friendly tool that provides keyword suggestions, search volume data, and difficulty scores.

- **Google Gemini**: Google's AI-driven tool that integrates with other Google services to provide detailed keyword insights and predictive analytics.

Methods for Performing Keyword Research

1. **Brainstorming and Initial Research**
2. Start by brainstorming a list of potential keywords related to your business and services. Consider what

your customers might search for and use tools like Google Suggest to get ideas.

3. **Using Keyword Research Tools**

- **Google Keyword Planner**: Enter your initial list of keywords to see search volumes, competition levels, and additional keyword suggestions.

- **AnswerThePublic**: Input a general topic to get a visual map of questions and phrases people are searching for related to that topic.

- **Keyword Surfer**: Install this Chrome extension to see keyword volumes directly in Google search results as you type your queries.

- **Google Search Console**: Analyze the performance of your existing keywords and discover new ones you're already ranking for but might have yet to target explicitly.

4. **Analyzing Competitor Keywords**

- **SEMrush and Ahrefs**: Use these tools to see which keywords your competitors are ranking for. Look for gaps where they rank well, but you don't, and consider targeting those keywords.

- **Moz Keyword Explorer**: Input your competitors' URLs to see their top-performing keywords and content.

5. **Refining Your List with User Intent**

6. Categorize your keywords based on user intent (informational, transactional, local). This helps you create content that directly addresses the needs of different search intents.

7. **Expanding with Long-Tail Keywords**

   - **Google Suggest and Related Searches**: Use Google's auto-suggestions and related searches at the bottom of the search results page to find long-tail keywords.

   - **Ubersuggest**: Enter a seed keyword with search volume and competition data to get long-tail keyword suggestions.

8. **Incorporating Semantic Keywords and Entities**

9. Use tools like **LSIGraph** or **Google's Natural Language API** to find semantically related terms and entities to include in your content, enriching your keyword strategy and improving relevance.

By mastering the art of keyword research, you can uncover the hidden language of your customers, create content that resonates with their needs, and ultimately drive more qualified traffic to your home service website. Remember, keyword research is an ongoing process, as language and search trends constantly evolve. Stay curious, experiment with different tools, and adapt your strategy to stay ahead of the curve.

Schema Markup

Structured data, or schema markup, is a form of microdata used to make your website better understandable to search engines. With schema markup, your search engine listings can be enhanced with rich snippets, enhancing their attractiveness and informativeness. It is possible to significantly increase visibility and click-through rates for home service companies by implementing the right schema types.

Key Schema Markups for Home Service Companies

Let's focus on the most applicable types of schema markup for home service businesses:

1. LocalBusiness Schema

2. Service Schema

3. FAQ Schema

4. Review Schema

5. Product Schema

6. Event Schema

LocalBusiness Schema

The LocalBusiness schema is essential for any home service company that serves a specific geographic area. This schema helps search engines display detailed information about your business directly in search results.

Key Properties:

- **@type:** LocalBusiness

- **name:** Your business name

- **address:** Your physical address, including street, city, state, and zip code

- **telephone:** Your business phone number

- **openingHours:** Business hours of operation

- **geo:** Latitude and longitude coordinates

Example:

```
{

  "@context": "https://schema.org",

  "@type": "LocalBusiness",

  "name": "Busy Bob's Plumbing",

  "address": {

    "@type": "PostalAddress",
```

```
    "streetAddress": "123 Main St",

    "addressLocality": "Chicago",

    "addressRegion": "IL",

    "postalCode": "60601"

  },

  "telephone": "+1-800-555-1234",

  "openingHours": "Mo,Tu,We,Th,Fr 09:00-17:00",

  "geo": {

    "@type": "GeoCoordinates",

    "latitude": "41.8781",

    "longitude": "-87.6298"

  }

}
```

Service Schema

Service schema allows you to specify the types of services your company offers. This helps search engines understand the range of services you provide.

Key Properties:

- **@type:** Service
- **serviceType:** The specific type of service offered

- **provider:** The name of the business providing the service

- **areaServed:** The geographic area where the service is available

Example:

```
{

 "@context": "https://schema.org",

 "@type": "Service",

 "serviceType": "Plumbing",

 "provider": {

  "@type": "LocalBusiness",

  "name": "Busy Bob's Plumbing"

 },

 "areaServed": {

  "@type": "Place",

  "name": "Chicago"

 }

}
```

FAQ Schema

The FAQ schema allows you to mark up questions and answers on your website to help search engines feature them directly in search results.

Example:

```
{
  "@context": "https://schema.org",
  "@type": "FAQPage",
  "mainEntity": [{
    "@type": "Question",
    "name": "How do I fix a leaky faucet?",
    "acceptedAnswer": {
      "@type": "Answer",
      "text": "First, turn off the water supply to the faucet. Then, disassemble the faucet to check for worn-out parts and replace them as needed."
    }
  }]
}
```

Review Schema

Review schema allows you to include customer reviews in your markup, which can be displayed in rich snippets in search results, enhancing credibility and attractiveness.

Example:

```
{

  "@context": "https://schema.org",

  "@type": "Review",

  "author": "Jane Doe",

  "datePublished": "2024-05-15",

  "reviewBody": "Great service! Fixed my leaky faucet quickly and professionally.",

  "reviewRating": {

    "@type": "Rating",

    "ratingValue": "5",

    "bestRating": "5"

  },

  "itemReviewed": {

    "@type": "LocalBusiness",

    "name": "Busy Bob's Plumbing"

  }
```

}

Product Schema

If you sell products directly on your site (e.g., plumbing supplies), product schema can help you showcase product details in search results.

Example:

```
{
  "@context": "https://schema.org",
  "@type": "Product",
  "name": "Water Heater",
  "description": "A high-efficiency water heater.",
  "sku": "WH123",
  "offers": {
    "@type": "Offer",
    "priceCurrency": "USD",
    "price": "499.99",
    "availability": "https://schema.org/InStock"
  }
}
```

Event Schema

If your business hosts events (e.g., free plumbing workshops), using event schema can help promote these events directly in search results.

Example:

```
{
  "@context": "https://schema.org",
  "@type": "Event",
  "name": "Free Plumbing Workshop",
  "startDate": "2024-06-01T10:00",
  "endDate": "2024-06-01T12:00",
  "eventAttendanceMode":
"https://schema.org/OfflineEventAttendanceMode",
  "location": {
    "@type": "Place",
    "name": "Community Center",
    "address": {
      "@type": "PostalAddress",
      "streetAddress": "456 Elm St",
      "addressLocality": "Chicago",
      "addressRegion": "IL",
```

```
    "postalCode": "60601"

  }

 }

}
```

Search engine visibility can be greatly improved by implementing schema markup on your website. Using the appropriate schema types for home service companies like LocalBusiness, Service, FAQ, Review, Product, and Event can significantly enhance how your business appears in search results. By doing so, search engines will understand your content better, making your listings more appealing and informative to potential customers. Add these schema markups to your site to boost your SEO efforts and attract more customers searching for your services.

Backlink Building Strategies

What Are Backlinks and Why They Matter

Imagine someone looking for a company to fix their dishwasher. They go to their local community Facebook group and ask for a recommendation, and they see a lot of people recommending Rob's Appliance Repair more than any other company. Who do you think they're going to call? They'd call Rob's Appliance Repair, of course. When a website links to yours, it's basically like having someone else vouching for your credibility, expertise, and relevance. For home service businesses, these endorsements are paramount as they significantly influence your search engine rankings. As you get more backlinks, your site will appear more authoritative to search engines, which means higher rankings and more organic traffic - those valuable clicks from customers actively looking for you.

Understanding Domain Authority (DA) and Domain Rank (DR)

Before delving into specific strategies, let's grasp two key metrics:

- **Domain Authority (DA):** Developed by Moz, DA is a predictive score (1-100) indicating how well a website could rank in the search engine results pages (SERPs). A higher score suggests a greater ability to rank due to factors like linking root domains and total links.

- **Domain Rank (DR):** Ahrefs' metric, also ranging from 1 to 100, measures a website's backlink profile strength. Higher DR means a more robust backlink profile.

Both DA and DR help you assess the quality of linking sites. Higher scores generally signal more reputable and valuable backlinks, which have a greater impact on your SEO efforts.

Effective Backlink Building Strategies for Home Service Businesses

1. **Get Listed on Warranty and Manufacturer Websites:** If your business provides warranty services or is an authorized service provider for specific brands, listings on their websites are pure gold. These sites typically have high DA/DR, making their backlinks a powerful boost for your SEO. Ensure your business is included on their "Find a Service Provider" page with a direct link to your website. This establishes you as a trusted expert in your field.

2. **Local Chamber of Commerce Profiles:** Joining and actively participating in your local Chamber of Commerce opens doors to valuable local backlinks. These organizations often have high authority within your geographic area, making their links highly relevant to your target audience. Craft a comprehensive profile on their website, showcasing

your services and including a prominent link to your own site. This bolsters your local SEO and fosters connections with other businesses and potential customers.

3. **Guest Blogging:** Sharing your expertise through guest posts on reputable industry blogs can earn you high-quality backlinks. Seek blogs with high DA/DR catering to your target audience. Craft informative articles relevant to your services, subtly weaving links to your website within the content or author bio.

4. **Sponsorships and Community Engagement:** Sponsoring local events or charities strengthens your community ties and offers opportunities for backlinks from event websites. These links enhance your local SEO and increase brand visibility. Additionally, participating in community activities can lead to mentions in local news articles, often accompanied by backlinks from reputable sources.

Local Business Directories

Listing your business in local online directories expands your reach and provides valuable backlinks that enhance your SEO. Prioritize well-established directories with good domain authority, such as Yelp, Angie's List, Nextdoor, and local-specific listings like "Best Plumbers in [Your City]." These platforms help potential customers find your services and improve your website's visibility in search engine results.

Key Directories for Home Service Companies

Here are some specific directories where home service companies should consider listing their business:

1. **Yelp**

   - **Description**: A widely used platform where customers can find and review local businesses.

   - **Benefits**: High domain authority, extensive reach, and trusted by users for business reviews.

2. **Angie's**

   - **Description**: Focuses on reviews of local service providers and offers verified customer feedback.

   - **Benefits**: High domain authority and trusted source for finding reputable home service companies.

3. **Nextdoor**

   - **Description**: A neighborhood-based platform where locals recommend and review businesses.

- **Benefits**: Targeted local audience, community trust, and excellent for local SEO.

4. **HomeAdvisor**

   - **Description**: Connects homeowners with local service professionals for various projects.

   - **Benefits**: High domain authority and a large user base looking for home services.

5. **Thumbtack**

   - **Description**: A platform that helps people find local professionals for different services.

   - **Benefits**: High domain authority and targeted at users seeking home services.

6. **Houzz**

   - **Description**: A home remodeling and design platform where users can find professionals and get ideas.

   - **Benefits**: High domain authority and focused on home improvement and design.

7. **Google Business Profile**

- **Description**: Google's platform for managing your business presence on Google Search and Maps.

- **Benefits**: Crucial for local SEO, helps you appear in local and map search results, and provides valuable insights.

8. **Bing Places for Business**

   - **Description**: Bing's counterpart to Google Business Profile for listing and managing your business.

   - **Benefits**: Enhances visibility on Bing search results and maps.

9. **Better Business Bureau (BBB)**

   - **Description**: Provides accreditation and customer reviews for businesses.

   - **Benefits**: High domain authority and trusted by users for business credibility.

10. **Local.com**

    - **Description**: A directory for finding local businesses and services.

    - **Benefits**: Enhances local SEO and provides a platform for customer reviews.

Listing your home service business in these local online directories expands your reach and provides valuable backlinks that improve your SEO. Prioritize directories with high domain authority and strong local relevance to maximize your visibility and attract more customers. Ensure your business information is consistent across all listings to enhance your local search performance and credibility. These platforms can help you get more leads to your website.

Press Releases: Generating Buzz and Building Links

Press releases offer a powerful way to announce noteworthy developments in your home service business, such as:

- **New Service Launches:** Introducing a new service or expanding your offerings.

- **Community Involvement:** Participating in charity events, sponsoring local initiatives, or receiving awards.

- **Company Milestones:** Celebrating anniversaries, achieving significant growth, or acquiring new certifications.

- **Partnerships:** Announcing collaborations with other businesses or organizations.

When you write good press releases and distribute them strategically, you can:

- **Earn Media Coverage:** Local news outlets and industry publications might pick up your story, increasing brand awareness and credibility.

- **Secure Backlinks:** News websites often link back to your website within the article, which boosts your SEO and online visibility.

- **Reach a Wider Audience:** Press release distribution services can amplify your reach, getting your news in front of a broader audience.

Crafting an Effective Press Release:

1. **Compelling Headline:** Grab attention with a concise, informative headline summarizing the main news.

2. **Dateline:** Include the city and state where the news originates.

3. **Lead Paragraph:** Summarize the most important information in the first paragraph (who, what, where, when, why).

4. **Body:** Provide additional details and context, highlighting the benefits or impact of the news.

5. **Quote:** Include a quote from a key person in your company, adding a personal touch and credibility.

6. **Boilerplate:** Briefly describe your company and its mission.

7. **Contact information:** Make it easy for journalists to contact you.

Distribution Strategies:

- **Local Media:** Target local newspapers, radio stations, TV channels, and online news outlets.

- **Industry Publications:** Identify relevant trade publications or blogs that cover your industry.

- **Press Release Distribution Services:** Consider using services like EIN Presswire, Cision, or PR Newswire to reach a wider audience.

- **Social Accounts:** Utilize social media to share your press release.

Example Template:

FOR IMMEDIATE RELEASE

[Your City, State] – [Date] – [Your Company Name], a leading provider of [your services] in [your area], today announced the launch of its new [new service]. This innovative service will help homeowners [benefits of the service].

"[Quote about the new service and its benefits]," said [Your Name], [Your Title] at [Your Company Name].

[Talk about your new service]

About [Your Company Name]

[Your Company Name] is a [brief company description].

Media Contact:[Your Name] [Your Title] [Your Email] [Your Phone Number]

Using press releases in your marketing strategy can help you gain valuable media exposure, boost your brand's digital presence, and build backlinks.

Citations

A citation is an online reference to your business' name, address, and phone number (NAP). These virtual breadcrumbs are scattered across the internet, helping potential customers find you and signaling to search engines that your business is legitimate and relevant to local searches.

Why Citations Matter for Home Service Businesses

- **Local SEO Boost:** When your NAP is consistently listed across reputable directories, search engines like Google gain confidence in your business's information. In your service area, this will help potential customers find you more easily when they need your services via local search results.

- **Increased Visibility:** Citation sites often have high domain authority, which means your listing there can attract more traffic to your website.

- **Building Trust:** Consistent citations build credibility. Customers who see your business mentioned on multiple reputable platforms are more likely to trust your services.

NAP Consistency is Key

The golden rule of citations is consistency. Every online mention of your business should have the exact same NAP information. Your local SEO efforts will be compromised if even minor discrepancies are present (e.g., "St." versus "Street").

Essential Citation Sites for Home Service Businesses

1. **The Core Four:**

   - **Google Business Profile:** This is your most critical citation. It powers your Google Maps listing and is often the first result people see in local searches.

   - **Bing Places:** While Google dominates, pay attention to Bing. Claim and optimize your listing here to reach a wider audience.

   - **Apple Maps:** This is essential if you want your business to show up in Apple Maps searches.

   - **Facebook:** Even if you don't actively use it for marketing, having a Facebook page with accurate NAP information is important for local SEO.

2. **Data Aggregators:**

   - **Data Axle (formerly Infogroup):** This is a major data provider for many online directories. Ensure your listing here is accurate, as it can impact your information across many platforms.

   - **Neustar Localeze:** Similar to Data Axle, Localeze feeds many other directories.

Correct information here is crucial for widespread accuracy.

- **Foursquare:** This platform provides a great opportunity to reach potential customers looking for businesses nearby.

3. **Industry-Specific Directories:**

- **HomeAdvisor:** A major platform for connecting homeowners with home service professionals.

- **Angi (formerly Angie's List):** Like HomeAdvisor, Angi offers home service reviews and ratings.

- **Yelp:** While not exclusively for home services, Yelp reviews can significantly influence consumer decisions.

- **Nextdoor:** This neighborhood-focused platform can be a great way to connect with potential clients in your local community.

4. **Other Important Directories:**

- **Better Business Bureau (BBB):** A strong BBB rating builds customer trust.

- **Yellow Pages:** While less popular now, Yellow Pages still hold some relevance, especially for older demographics.

- **Chamber of Commerce (Local):** A listing here shows your commitment to your community and can boost your local credibility.

- **Industry-specific niche directories:** Research directories that cater specifically to your type of home service (e.g., electrician directories, plumbing directories).

Pro Tips for Citation Building

- **Prioritize Quality Over Quantity:** Focus on getting listed on the most authoritative and relevant sites first.

- **Use a Citation Tool:** Citation management tools like Moz Local, BrightLocal, or Whitespark can help you manage your citations more effectively.

- **Regularly Audit Your Citations:** Make it a habit to check your listings for accuracy and consistency.

- **Content Marketing:** Make your website a source of high-quality, useful content that others will naturally link to. This could include blog posts, how-to guides, infographics, or videos related to your home services. Using email marketing and social media to share this content can definitely increase visibility and backlinks.

The process of building a strong backlink profile takes time. Never take the spray-and-pray approach. It requires consistent effort over time and a focus on quality over quantity. By strategically targeting high-authority websites, engaging with your community, and creating valuable content, you can build a network of backlinks that propels your home service business to the top of search results, attracting more customers and driving sustainable growth.

Keeping Pace with Algorithm Updates

Search engine algorithms constantly evolve, with updates rolled out regularly to improve search quality and relevance. Staying informed about these updates and adjusting your SEO strategies accordingly is required for maintaining your home service business's online visibility and search rankings.

Monitoring Algorithm Changes and Updates

In order to stay ahead of the curve, you need to be vigilant and have access to reliable resources. Here are some essential tools and platforms to help you monitor algorithm updates:

1. **Google Search Status Dashboard: https://status.search.google.com/summary**

   Google's official dashboard provides real-time updates on the status of various Google Search services, including crawling, indexing, ranking, and new updates. While it doesn't explicitly announce algorithm changes ahead of time, it does display when an update is rolled out.

2. **Semrush Sensor: https://www.semrush.com/sensor/**

   This tool by Semrush tracks volatility in Google's search results across different industries and regions. Significant fluctuations often indicate algorithm updates, allowing you to investigate further and adjust your strategies if necessary.

3. **MozCast: https://moz.com/mozcast**

4. This "weather report" for Google's algorithm visually represents daily fluctuations in search results. A "stormy" forecast could suggest an algorithm update is underway.

5. **SERP   Seismometer: https://www.similarweb.com/serp/**

6. This tool analyzes search engine results pages (SERPs) to identify potential risks and opportunities related to algorithm changes. It provides insights into which keywords and industries are most affected by recent updates.

7. **X: https://x.com/searchliaison**

8. Follow Google's Search Liaison (@searchliaison) and other prominent SEO experts on X to receive real-time updates and insights on algorithm changes.

Responding to Algorithm Updates

When an algorithm update is confirmed:

1. **Don't Panic:** It's important to realize that traffic and rankings naturally fluctuate during an algorithm update. As long as you have followed SEO best practices, you shouldn't have anything to worry about. I have found in most cases, if you monitor things and just wait until the rollout is complete, you'll see things start to stabilize. Once your rankings are stabilized, you can then, and only then, make an informed decision if changes need to be made. Algorithm updates can take anywhere from 1 week to 45 days to completely roll out.

2. **Assess the Impact:** Analyze your website's traffic and rankings to determine if you've been affected.

3. **Identify the Cause:** Research the update to understand what factors it focuses on and how it might have impacted your site.

4. **Adjust Your Strategy:** Make necessary changes to your SEO strategy to align with the updated algorithm's requirements.

5. **Monitor and Adapt:** Continuously monitor your website's performance and be prepared to make further adjustments as needed.

In order to keep your home service business competitive in an ever-evolving landscape, it is vital that you monitor algorithm updates regularly and adjust your SEO strategies as soon as necessary. Doing so will ensure that your business has a competitive edge as the search engines continue to evolve.

CHAPTER

14

A CASE STUDY OF SUCCESS

Once upon a time in Lexington, Kentucky, there was a guy named EJ who ran a small but earnest appliance repair business. EJ was no stranger to the marketing grind; he had been slogging it out with another marketing firm for almost a year. His website design was terrible, leads weren't coming in, and his Google Ad campaigns were underperforming. Unfortunately, as anyone with a beating heart would know, that partnership didn't quite pan out.

EJ was left feeling like he was spinning his wheels without getting anywhere. He had just gone all in on his business and wanted to hire a new technician. He had little hope that things would change when he decided to hire ApplianceMarketingPros.com, but boy, was he in for a surprise.

The Challenge:

EJ's previous marketing firm had left him with a subpar website and a serious lack of results. His expectations were low when he approached Mike Carson at ApplianceMarketingPros.com, but he figured he had nothing to lose. His primary needs were a new website, SEO services, and effective Google Ads management.

The transformation and a good story

My team and I jumped in the deep end right away. We just had to help EJ and show him what a real marketing agency was made of. Within a few weeks, we had built a brand-new, SEO-optimized website that blew EJ's old site out of the water. The new site was packed with content, photos, and all the SEO bells and whistles that make a site look good and perform well in search engines.

Our team then turned to the off-page SEO strategies outlined in this book. EJ's site started climbing to the first page of Google extremely fast. To be totally transparent, he had nowhere to go but up.

In the first 3 months, EJ's new website ranked on page 1 for 165 keywords we were tracking, all of which had notable search volume. And out of those 165 keywords, about 50% of them were in the top 3 results. I remember that 3 months into our campaign, EJ sent a Facebook message and couldn't believe he was in the number 1 spot for his most valued keyword.

Then, at almost our 6th month into the year, EJ sent a message saying that he had already grossed just over the same sales as he did the prior year. I was elated to be part of such a huge business transformation.

But that's not the best part, at least for me. When we were about 5 months into the campaign, I attended an appliance repair event in Atlanta, GA. Ej was there with his two techs, Terry and 5 Star Mike. A group of us went to dinner, and EJ sat across the table from me. 5-Star Mike was sitting on my right side, and we had only been introduced by name up to that point. He seemed like the kind of guy that you wouldn't want to piss off, so I figured I'd just keep to myself. Well, EJ and I started talking shop and about the marketing stuff. Suddenly, 5-star Mike jumps out of his chair and stands up with a super intimidating stance. I didn't know what this guy was going to do. He said to me, "You're the marketing guy? I wanna shake your hand! Before you came along, I didn't know if I'd even have a job from week to week."

It's statements like this that give us purpose at our agency. And it turned out that 5-Star Mike was not just EJ's employee; he was also EJ's pastor and turned out to be a great guy, and I am happy to now call him my friend.

Testimonial:

Here's EJ in his own words:

"Hey everybody, EJ here from EJ's Appliance Repair in Lexington, Kentucky. I wanted to give a little shout out to Mike Carson and ApplianceMarketingPros.com. I hired Mike in December to take over my SEO marketing and Google advertising. Within about two to three weeks, he had a website built that far exceeded what I had before—several pages, lots of content, pictures, everything that I needed. That website is ejsappliances.com. So, January 6 we went live. If you know about the appliance repair industry, that's the slow season, and it was slow, but we stayed alive for those two months. That was my transition from going part-time as a business owner to full-time. By March, we had doubled our gross sales in my business. We got so busy after just two months that I had to start looking at hiring another guy.

I have since hired another tech to cover the area that I was trying to grow in. I now have a second tech training to take over that area as well. Within just less than six months, a new website ranking number one organically on Google for several search terms, almost all of them that matter, and we are having our phone ring off the hook. I had to hire a call center, My Office Help, to answer my calls because for my one CSR, my wife, it became way too much. These are good problems to have, and these are the ones I asked for. I asked Mike Carson to deliver, and that is exactly what he did. So I thank you for all the problems I now have, Mike. These are much better problems than I had before. Thank you."

The Results:

The results speak for themselves. EJ's Appliance Repair saw a staggering 140% growth within the first year of working with ApplianceMarketingPros.com. The new SEO-optimized website, SEO, and effective Google Ads management played a vital role in this transformation. EJ went from barely hanging on to hiring additional staff to keep up with the demand.

EJ's new online presence also contributed to his company winning first place for the 2022 Most Professional Servicer award in his category.

Lessons Learned and Best Practices

So, what did we learn from EJ's story? Here are a few key takeaways:

1. **Don't Settle for Mediocre Marketing:**

   - If your current marketing firm isn't delivering results, it's time to move on. A fresh perspective and a dedicated team can make all the difference.

2. **Invest in a Quality Website:**

   - A well-designed, SEO-optimized website is a game-changer. It's about more than just looking good; it's about performing well in search engines and converting visitors into customers.

3. **SEO and PPC Go Hand in Hand:**

   - Combining SEO with effective Google Ads management can drive both organic and paid traffic, leading to sustained growth.

4. **Adapt to Growth:**

   - Be prepared to adapt to increased demand. EJ had to hire additional staff and a call center to handle the influx of business—good problems to have!

5. **Continuous Improvement:**

    - SEO and digital marketing are more than one-time efforts. Continuous monitoring, tweaking, and optimizing are crucial for maintaining and improving results.

EJ's Appliance Repair is a testament to what can happen when you partner with the right marketing team and invest in your online presence. So, if you're feeling stuck like EJ once did, remember that transformation is possible—sometimes, all it takes is the right push.

If you'd like to be one of our many success stories, go to the following URL, and let's get on a strategy call to see how we can help you grow your business just like EJ did.

https://appliancemarketingpros.com/schedule

CHAPTER

15

NEXT STEPS

Throughout this book, we've covered an abundance of information—so much so that you're probably ready to start your own digital marketing agency! We've mapped out your internet marketing plan and taken you step-by-step through how to claim and optimize your Google Business Profile, optimize your website for the most commonly searched keywords in your area, and leverage social media to get more repeat and referral business. We also dove into paid online marketing strategies like pay-per-click (PPC) and pay-per-lead (PPL) services. If you've taken action and followed our instructions, you should be well on your way to dominating the search engines for the keywords in your area.

But wait, there's more! Just like those late-night infomercials, we're not done yet. Here's how to keep the momentum going.

Need More Help?

If you've gotten to this point and need extra help to implement these ideas, don't worry. We're here to support you. As experts in helping home service businesses nationwide, we've had tremendous success implementing these strategies. Whether you're feeling overwhelmed, stuck, or just want to make sure you're on the right track, we've got your back.

You can schedule your Lead Flow Strategy Session at the following URL:

https://appliancemarketingpros.com/schedule

- **Reach Out for Personalized Assistance:** You can contact us through our website at https:// appliancemarketingpros.com or call us directly at 1-888-760-0878 with any questions. Our team of experts will analyze your entire online marketing campaign (website, competitors, search engine placement, social media, etc.) and present a complete evaluation of what you can do to improve and grow your online marketing efforts.

- **Stay Updated:** Digital marketing is constantly evolving. Keep up with industry news by following thought leaders on YouTube, social media, participating in webinars, and subscribing to industry newsletters. Continuous learning is key to staying competitive.

- **Final point:** Keep in mind that digital marketing is a continuous process that requires regular tweaks and adjustments. Apply the strategies we discussed, measure your results, and iterate based on the results.

You now have the tools and knowledge to significantly improve your home service business's online visibility. The journey may seem daunting sometimes, but you can achieve remarkable results with persistence, creativity, and the right strategies. So go ahead, take that leap, and watch your business grow!

Thank you for taking this journey with me. I look forward to seeing your success and am always here to help when you need it. Happy marketing!

CHAPTER

16

APPENDICES

Let's conclude with a selection of invaluable free resources that will propel your digital marketing journey. Whether you're in need of checklists, resources for guidance, or a supportive community, I've got you covered with resources that can significantly enhance your online visibility and marketing strategies.

Mike's Free Resources

I believe in giving back to the community and helping home service business owners thrive. Below are some free resources and channels for additional support and information.

Digital Marketing Checklist

This comprehensive checklist covers all the essential steps to ensure your digital marketing strategy is on point.

- https://appliancemarketingpros.com/marketing-checklist

Ultimate Google Business Profile Optimization Checklist for home Service Business

Optimize your Google Business Profile with this detailed checklist to improve your local SEO.

- https://appliancemarketingpros.com/gbp-checklist

Local Marketing Lounge Facebook Group

Step into a vibrant community of home service business owners, all united in their quest for digital marketing excellence. Share insights, pose questions, and find the support you need to thrive.

- https://www.facebook.com/groups/localmarketin glounge

Local Marketing Lounge Podcast (YouTube)

Stay ahead of the digital marketing game by subscribing to our YouTube channel. Our videos are packed with insights tailored to your needs, covering topics such as digital marketing and SEO.

- https://www.youtube.com/@ApplianceMarketingPros

Service Alliance Group Podcast (YouTube)

Tune into the Service Alliance Group Podcast for valuable discussions and insights into the home service industry.

- https://www.youtube.com/c/servicealliancepodcast

Join our mailing list

By joining our mailing list, you can stay up to date with the latest local marketing tips, strategies, and news in digital marketing that matter for your home service business. Sign up on our website.

- https://appliancemarketingproscom/mailing-list

Visit Our Blog

Our blog is loaded with articles on various digital marketing topics. It's a great resource for ongoing learning.

- https://appliancemarketingpros.com/blog

Follow Us On Facebook

Get updates and tips, and engage with our content by following our official Facebook page.

- https://www.facebook.com/ApplianceMarketingPros

www.ingramcontent.com/pod-product-compliance
Lightning Source LLC
LaVergne TN
LVHW051638050326
832903LV00022B/799